SAVING
SAILING

SAVING SAILING

*The Story of Choices,
Families, Time Commitments,
and How We Can Create
a Better Future*

NICHOLAS D. HAYES

CRICKHOLLOW BOOKS

Crickhollow Books is an imprint of Great Lakes Literary, LLC,
of Milwaukee, Wisconsin, an independent press working to create
books of lasting quality.

Our titles are available from your favorite bookstore.
For a complete catalog of all our titles or to place special orders:

www.CrickhollowBooks.com

Saving Sailing
© 2009, Nicholas Dale Hayes

Foreword © 2009, William Schanen III

Cover artwork is by Curt Crain (http://www.crainpainting.com).

For more, visit the *Saving Sailing* book website and blog:
www.savingsailing.com

Publisher's Cataloging-in-Publication Data
(Prepared by The Donohue Group, Inc.)

    Hayes, Nicholas D.
      Saving sailing : the story of choices, families, time commitments,
    and how we can create a better future / Nicholas D. Hayes ; [fore-
    word by William Schanen III].

      p. ; cm.

    Includes bibliographical references.
    ISBN: 978-1-933987-07-1

    1. Sailing – United States. 2. Sailing – United States – History.
    3. Outdoor recreation – United States. 4. Family recreation
    – United States. 5. Family – United States – 20th century.
    6. Leisure counseling – United States. I. Title.

GV811 .H39 2009
797.124/0973

Original Trade Softcover
Printed in Canada

Note
....

With a few identified exceptions, the people, places and events in these stories are not real. However, they are based on the stories of real people, told about actual places and events, assembled here to make a point.

Acknowledgements

I've felt the embrace of many families who have helped me to find joy in this life and for whom I write this book, notably the Terranovas, the Peters, the Schanens, the Depoy-Singers, the Wozniaks, and of course the Hayes family.

I receive unconditional love, the Grandest Benefit, from my parents, Paul and Philia, and from my brother John and his family, Mira, Paul, and Kane.

I live here with an angel, Angela, who chose to share her time on earth with me and gave me the greatest gifts, Kate and Elizabeth, and from whom I humbly receive these lessons.

I consider many of my sailing crew-mates to be brothers and sisters. They include: Jackie Beltz, Don Ellingsen, Jake Gerlach, Catherine Hackbarth, Jamie Hummert, Tim Kent, Pat McMahon, Sébastien Motte, Eric Persha, Dale Peters, Susan Sorce Rieck, Eric Roman, Tim Roy, Bill Schanen III, Jean Schanen, Erin Schanen, Bill Schanen IV, Brad Slusar, and Steve and Roxanne Terranova.

There are many other sailors and friends who helped inform this story. They include John Achim, Lisa Alberte, Bob and Fran Aring, Mike Bersch, Pete Brothers, Dean Cady, Curt Crain, Holly Davenport, Stephanie and Jared Drake, Joe Fillingham, Phil Fons, the Freysinger-Beck family, Danny Gautraud, Bill Goggins, Chris Gribble, Brian Hancock, Peter and Olaf Harken, Sally Heuer, Dan Herda, Joe Horan, James Hutchison, the Kent/Jones clan, John Kretschmer, Barb Kueny, the Kinneys, Jane Larson, Laura and Glyn Livermore, Phyllis McDonald, the McMahon family, Emil Meucci, Art Mitchell, Bill Mosher, Cookie Mueller, Alistair Murray, Erin Noyes, Tom Pease, Ella Pienovich, Ken Quant, Marty Rieck, Peter Rieck, the Reiske family, Torsten Ringberg, the Sabinash family, the Schroeder family, John Strassman, Scot Tempesta, Jim Vaudreuil, Chad Vollmer, Russ Whitford, Mark Wildhagen, Billy Willman, Juli Wood, Tony Wood, Andy Wright and the members of the Milwaukee Community Sailing Center and the Milwaukee and South Shore Yacht Clubs.

Thanks also to Karl Kirkman, Naval Architect and former member of the America's Cup technology team, for his insights into the first America's Cup race.

Contents

PART TWO

PART THREE

Foreword

by Bill Schanen, Sailing Magazine

Nick Hayes is in love with sailing.

I knew that before I read it in this book, having sailed as skipper of an offshore racing sailboat on which he was a key member of the crew. That was some years ago, but I remember well the intensity of his commitment to our effort and the evident joy he derived from the panoply of intense experiences sailing produces. Later I watched as he bought his own boat and shared like experiences with his wife and two little daughters (who have since grown into confident, skilled young sailing women). So I'm not surprised he had to ask the question: Why isn't sailing, the activity that has given his family so much pleasure amid the glorious aesthetics of the sea, the most irresistible pastime in the world?

In his pursuit of the answer, the first thing Nick learned was that sailing is anything but irresistible: Participation in sailing in the United States has declined by about 40% in the last decade. Trying to make sense of that resulted in this book, a fast-moving intellectual voyage that takes readers to some unexpected stops along the way but ends in a place that is familiar and intuitively right.

Lack of time to make a commitment to sailing is the problem, or so said many people Nick interviewed. Yet he found that Americans, hard working though we may be, have plenty of time for non-working activities. Claims on that time, often by sources we can't control, are the real problem, personified by what has become an American cliché: Parents with young children functioning as schedulers and taxi drivers delivering their children to a calendar-filling round of organized activities that keep their kids amused but leave little time for meaningful family experiences.

It has long been an axiom of the sailing world that the way to build lifelong participation is to give children sailing instruction at a young age. And so for some families, sailing lessons become one more mini-van stop. The kids are put in small boats, often one-person Optimist dinghies; they learn a little bit about sailing, have some fun, and then get picked up for the next soccer practice or Little League game. Few children grow up to be baseball or soccer players, and very few grow up to be sailors. Most graduates of youth sailing programs do not become adult sailors.

Saving Sailing makes the case that the way to get around the barriers that inhibit the growth of sailing is to return to an ancient building block of civilization that seems to have gone missing in the 21st century: mentoring. Experiences shared in a family or an amalgamation of friends or other group, with the skills and appreciation of the activity passed on from mentors to aspiring mentors, are the foundation of pastimes that endure for lifetimes. Nick writes about sailing in this context, but what he calls the mentoring continuum goes far beyond that, and it is more important than merely deriving pleasure from a pastime. Mentoring is nothing less than the key to making more valuable use of the time we are allotted for our lives.

Nick Hayes guides us to a conclusion that floats on a buoyant platform of instantly recognizable common sense, yet leaves us wanting to shout, "Eureka! Why didn't I think of that?" And wanting to go sailing with friends . . . right now.

Bill Schanen
Editor and Publisher
Sailing Magazine

Introduction

Meet fourth-grader Abigail, Sailor, and consider child-hood lessons, and a bit about this book.

A BIGAIL WAS EXCITED ABOUT the spring sailing field-trip. She loved the lake, and she loved sailing. She knew that others probably wouldn't understand how she felt so she took a book for company, just in case.

The schooner crew helped the kids and the three parent chaperones snug bulky orange lifejackets, and had them sit in three rows on the foredeck while the boat motored out onto the open water from behind the break-wall. They asked for volunteers to haul halyards, and three kids and a dad got in the line and pretended to pull while making pirate noises. There wasn't enough wind to sail, so the exercise was more show than substance. The sails limply flogged while the boat motored in a big circle tour.

Abigail saw what she was looking for. She excitedly tugged the teacher's sleeve, pointed off the port bow and said, "Mister Spaythe, sometimes I can almost touch that buoy light with my toes. Mom says it's the finest place on earth, so I am going to try and try until I do." Spaythe tried hard to digest what she was saying. Abigail continued with excitement, "Me and my brother stick our feet out from the rail after we take down the kite and they trim sails and we head up." Spaythe, now lost in the strange vocabulary and distracted by three spitting boys, concluded that it must be a child's fantasy. He said, "Nice, Abigail nice," and went to separate the boys.

Early childhood lessons from many sources tell us that sailing is something that other people do. We watch passively while someone recreates a sailing adventure. And we're told that the water and weather are dangerous and should be avoided.

We learn about treacherous and deadly waves and wind, sharks and pirates, sudden violent hurricanes, and foul-mouthed drunken men. Myths mostly, like the sure disaster of swimming too soon after eating. For the vast majority of Americans, the idea of fun on the water in a sailing boat seems so risky and foreign that they will never try. Since so few of us are sailors, and the rest of the population doesn't understand basic sailing ideas, the average person doesn't have much opportunity to hear a counterpoint.

As we are about to see, sailing is not risky or inaccessible in the ways that we often think.

Some of us, like fourth-grader Abigail and me, do end up going out in boats, as often as we can. Given a myriad of options, many which seem safer and more productive, some less expensive, and most more comfortable, we choose to spend big blocks of our life on earth on sailboats, in fishing skiffs or duck-blinds, in rehearsal halls or gardens — in some place banded together doing in an activity that we think is our touchpoint with the world and the people we share it with.

This book explains the decline of sailing and by association other group activities that, for a time, shaped the lives of many American families.

We're going to explore how we decide to spend our time: where we go, what we do, and who we do it with. In the process, we will begin to understand how our choices matter.

I will present a case that the way we use our free time has enormous consequences for us, the people around us, and potentially for the generations that follow. I will show that people — men, women and children — who choose to fill their time with complex, learned group activities like sailing live longer, happier, healthier and more satisfying lives than those who cannot, do not or will not. In this exploration, we will not be concerned with the number of people that sail, but with how we go about it, and what it means in terms of social impact. We will focus on the consequences of the decisions we make for us and for our inner and outer social circles.

Along the way, you will meet some composite characters, built from more than a thousand interviews that I conducted with sailors and would-be sailors in roughly a six-year period between 2003 and 2009.

We will use their experiences to create a short history of sailing as a pastime. We will distinguish between the needs and the approaches of the most active sailors, the newcomers and people looking in from the outside. We will show how and why some benefit and why some don't. We will look at how a pastime like sailing can be broadly popular and then appear to flame out within a generation. We will explore how a group with a deep common interest can miss out on opportunities to strengthen itself.

Then we will turn and face into the wind, so to speak. How will pastime choices change and matter for the next generations of Americans? Can we begin to set new, modern priorities for our available time that will have an impact not just on sailing but on our view of life and prosperity?

A note of full personal disclosure: I like to sail. However, I also like to hunt, hike, write, sing, work, bike and go to museums. This is not a call to choose one activity over another; it is not a stunt to promote sailing.

I have no desire to judge people's choices or claim one to be better or best. For all practical purposes, I could make the case using fishing or knitting or playing an instrument, or any other activity that brings us joy by helping us to pass on what we know and love about life.

Instead, we will consider if these active pastimes will soon be just an aberration in our social history, like men with powdered wigs, communal barn raisings or free love. And we will find out if sailing, and things like it, might matter in the future, in ways that we may not be able to predict, but can affect, through changes today.

What are those changes? Should we try to save sailing? If so, to what end?

Part One

*What sailing is
and how it came to be.*

CHAPTER 1

Sailing Looks Forward and Backward

Some find sailing to be magnetic, consuming, even spiritual. It is meaning. It is connection, both forward and backward and inward and outward. It is part of a belief system.

ONE OUT OF FIVE times, the wind will die before the Wednesday evening sailboat race finishes. On this night the water turned glassy-gray before the last puffs of a high breeze were spent. There was just enough wind left to hold a race, and forty boats were all trying to grab their share.

While we had had a terrible back-of-the-pack start, our light boat in these conditions would give us a good chance to come back. We stayed even on the first and second legs. Then on the third and final leg, far in front of us, spinnakers collapsed, windless. We had the benefit of the hindsight of the fleet and decided that if we "heated up"[1] we would be able stay in the remaining zephyrs and the extra distance would pay off in progress that nobody else would make.

We adjusted the big green spinnaker and ghosted above and around the fleet, clawing inch by inch back into contention. Every so often the boat found enough speed to outrun the wind and we teetered on the edge of a stall.

Silent concentration exposed a twitchy excitement as our comeback built. It was a long time sitting on a damp cold deck on a damp cold night. Relegated to positions on the low side of the boat near the water away from the action and blind behind the sails, the foredeck team chatted about the sandwiches waiting at the dock.

The kite[2] sagged lifeless just as John asked Angela if she had packed sub sauce or mayonnaise and mustard for condiments.

Sensing distraction, my daughter Elizabeth, the nine-year-old on station at the runners[3], barked, "Why are we

---

1 In sailing jargon, "heating up" is slang, meaning to decrease the steered angle relative to the wind direction (which increases the lifting potential of the sail and increases speed).

2 "Kite" is sailing slang for spinnaker.

talking about sub sauce? Come on, people! Keep your heads in the game. We are *racing* here!"

The crew snapped into sheepish focus, and we went on to finish in second place. Elizabeth got the MVP award for the night.

Sailing connects us with our future.

Papou's gaze was distant as the old boat puttered past the last river lighthouse and coughed diesel fumes onto greenish-brown Lake Michigan open water. He had moved his possessions and my Alzheimer's-stricken grandmother to Wisconsin to live out their last years closer to his daughter, my mother. As an outing, daughters and grandsons thought it would be good to spend a couple of hours on a sailing tour-boat plying the cool bay in June.

We paid six bucks each and then wheeled Yiayia in her chair up the ramp and found a spot out of the way to park and set the brake. Then we helped Papou shuffle to a tattered vinyl seat on the aft deck.

---

3 Runners are lines that hold up the mast and are reset from one side to the other, depending on the boat's angle to the wind.

Aisle markers, flood lights and restroom signs disclosed this boat's utility: it was for rides, not for work, races or adventures. But when the old sail rose and the engine stopped, she set onto a slow, lazy path east and gave her passengers time to think.

Papou wept openly for almost two hours, the duration of the tour. He was seven thousand miles and seventy years away from the small Greek sailing boats on the Aegean, but he was close enough. It was special for him in ways that I was just starting to understand.

Sailing, even in its shallowest likeness, has the power to durably connect us with our past.

A stiff southerly had built overnight, pushing big rain before it, with low gray clouds and a frothy sea. We had been cruising for a week, slowly making our way south from Mackinac Island after the big race, stopping at pretty ports like Harbor Springs and Leland to swim, dine and explore. We needed to get back to work, and our final passage, ninety miles across the lake, would be intense given the weather.

Under full main and a small jib, the powerful racing sloop locked onto a screaming wet beam-reach[4] straight west, gliding up and down the backs of the big waves, shuddering and then accelerating to slice the face of the next ridge. Every so often, spray would break the deck and fire-hose the crew. Less often but with far more power, a big green wave would reach many feet over the bow and roll down the deck to the stern, shoving us all backward on the way.

Driving was a delight. I did as much as my shoulders and triceps and the skipper would allow, and when he reclaimed the helm, I scurried up to sit on the rail next to my wife, spent. I pulled up my hood and secured the strings and rolled my fingers around my thumbs inside my jacket pockets.

Ninety minutes later, someone nudged me aware. I have a vague memory of being attached to a long and low rhythm, hypnotized by the white noise from the trailing wave, dreaming faces in the clouds and flames on the waves, and sensing the nature gods swirling in the big, boisterous breeze.

---

4 A beam reach is the point of sail at which the wind direction is approximately perpendicular to the boat. It feels fast.

ᔄ

Sailing has the potential to connect us with our souls. In fact, sailing takes some of us as close to God as we think we might ever be.

God, through sailing? Such a claim might seem unbelievable to non-sailors, but the premise comes clear when you consider what is happening when we are sailing.

First, the physics: We rig a sleek, lightweight canoe with enormous wings, some that face up into the sky and some that face down into the sea. We listen to our senses and nature's cues. We point things in roughly the right direction and are always awed when pure, free, invisible solar power grants us forward motion. Impressive speeds require tiny bits of energy, and sailboats use what they get very efficiently, leaving absolutely no waste or wake.

It is an engineering marvel, a scheme to trick water and air to cooperate to give motion. A sailboat is so good at it that it can approach the possibility of perpetual motion. Tuned right, a sailboat can go on forever. Set the sails, lock the tiller and stand down. Some cross oceans this way.

But a sailboat needs people to go well, and then it seems to come to life. Small adjustments and constant care from teams return comfort, safety and speed.

And so, physics give way to the psychology: The sailor

at the helm feels both directed by nature and, for a time, an anointed director of a privileged, natural state. Sailors seek what they call "a groove" — a few moments, occasionally hours, where the boat is precisely balanced and the driver's concentration follows only water and wind.

On bigger boats sailed by groups, the groove comes only when the boat and the team are in perfect balance. Through their work, a sailboat's passengers share rich, lasting emotional connections on par with the mingling of singers in a gospel choir or players in a jazz quartet. It is no coincidence that jazz players also seek a "groove," a mix of rhythm, melody and riff that falls into place, and feels right, then and there. Once sailors or jazz musicians find their groove, they are almost certainly addicted. It can be organic, mystical, erotic, magical and musical all at once.

Unfortunately, in the last ten years, Americans have abruptly stopped sailing. Participation is down more than 40% since 1997 and 70% since 1979. Less than 1% of Americans remain self-described sailors. They are doing less of it and are enlisting fewer newcomers. Current economics are not helping.

Why is something as rich, substantial and significant to the people that do it facing such trouble?

Of course, sailing is not alone in this downturn. Participation in many activities that yield rich personal and cultural rewards, whether the aforementioned "groove" or strong interpersonal connections, is on a precipitous decline. To find out why, let's explore what activities like sailing mean to us culturally, economically and personally.

Let us start with basic age demographics. The average self-described American sailor is a white male, 40.1 years old. But that average age is deceiving. The largest (43%) age group of sailors are 55 and older. The average age of a sailboat owner is 54.8 years old.[5] The ratio of men to women is about seven to one.

There is a meager bubble (13%) of young sailors between 15 and 24 years old, both girls and boys. However when today's sailors reach 25 they generally quit. So proportionately, almost nobody between 25 and 44 is sailing.

U.S. Sailing Participation by Age Group	
Age group	Percentage
Over 65	12%
55-64	31%
45-54	19%
35-44	9%
25-34	8%
14-24	13%
Under 13	8%

Table 1. 2006-7 Primary Research of American Sailors
Number of Respondents: 1185

Sailing was and remains a favorite activity of the oldest boomers. Compared with U.S. census data, the average sailor is older than the general population by about 11 years, so the decline of sailing precedes boomer retirement and death by about a decade.

A crucial fact: key age groups that might sustain the activity — kids under 13, women and early parents — are essentially not sailing at all. From the basic population data, it is easy to conclude that unless sailing can soon attract newcomers in all age groups under about 40, from all genders and a wider range of income levels — something that it is not doing well today — the future of the activity is bleak.

Again, sailing is not alone in this trend. The U.S. census does not indicate near-term growth in overall participation in much of anything, due to the enormous population imbalance between the baby-boomer generation and the generations that follow it.

Consider that the number of people between 30 and 45 years of age has declined during the last 10 years by 15 percent. Meanwhile, the number of people who have surpassed the age of 51 has increased by 25 percent.

....

5 "2006–07 Research of American Sailors," Author's Primary Research. Number of respondents: 1,185.

We are beginning to see related signs of this population shift across the board: in participation reductions in overall church attendance, charitable giving, membership in social clubs, and many other areas where people gather to do things together. Given these facts, we can project with high confidence that in 2030, there will be fewer sailors — even if sailing remains attractive to the same percentage of the population.

Demographic trends hide an important truth: despite the numbers, there are modest actions that can be taken. Basic decisions can be made by individuals or within small groups to improve the situation, to slow or reverse the downward trend.

Perhaps we can save sailing if we start on a personal, family and community level. In the following chapters you will find some ideas, presented through stories involving people and their day-by-day choices.

CHAPTER 2

Ron Buys a Sailboat

At least thirty million Americans have been on a sailboat sometime in the last twenty years. Most took a ride. Every year, a few of them try to turn the experience into something more, and often they run into a wall.

R ON LIVES IN THE Finger Lakes Region in upstate New York because it is where he is employed but also because, as his wife Jeanne explains, "We both need to be near the water. It's in our blood." Ron listened to his dad's Navy stories while growing up. Those images and Jeanne's Irish heritage call them there. Ron is an engineer and Jeanne a part-time speech pathologist and stay-at-home mom of two.

On a March Florida vacation, the family opted for the combo snorkeling-and-sailing afternoon trip from a rack of activities brochures, and boarded the catamaran-turned-diveboat with suits and sunscreen and eighteen other pale northern vacationers. The sailboat motored from Key Largo to the famous John Pennekamp Coral Reef State Park, a few miles offshore. After a couple hours of snorkeling around the sunken Jesus statue and the docile barracuda, the crew set sail, and the catamaran leapt to life and charged home as the sun set. Memory made. Wow.

A month later, Ron proposed at dinner that they should offer $5400 for a 20-year-old J-24[6] sailboat for sale in a local boatyard. He highlighted the sunny warm leisure of the charter, promised weekends in the sun and harbored secret hopes of entering a local race. The kids squealed their approval. Jeanne was not sure, but the moment won and the next week Ron wrote checks for the boat, the registration and winter storage. He also charged new dock-lines and fenders, four new lifejackets, a GPS, and a summer slip on the lake to his VISA. Checks and charges totaled about $9800.

Still worth it, he thought.

Ron subscribed to three magazines and scanned the

----

6 A J-24 is a 24-foot fiberglass keelboat from the late 1970s with room for four or five people. Hundreds are sailed in races and on day-sails all over the U.S.

blogs and forums daily, reading about sail-trim, the latest gear and trailer-sailing vacations. Mostly he studied articles on boat preparation and care. Between business trips in May, Ron took a day off work to grind off three years of toxic blue bottom paint. He could not afford a weekend, because he had committed to coaching Sam's little league team and mandatory practices had begun. He wedged himself between the trailer bed and the hull, just enough room to hold his new belt sander. Two weeks and three fake sick-days later, he had zinc acrylate coating his nostrils and a new coat of copper and Teflon paint applied except where the trailer support pads met the hull.

The local J-24 champ walked by, ran a finger along the new paint, and told Ron he had ruined the boat, because the sander was not the orbital type and the paper was too coarse. It would never be competitive again, he said.

Still worth it, Ron thought.

Memorial Day would be the christening. The forecast was for rain, but that would not stop him. He made the sandwiches and packed the backpack. He had ordered new pairs of fingerless sailing gloves from an online outfitter for everyone, and he handed them out at breakfast.

On the third pull the starter line snapped. Ron tried to recoil it but gashed his thumb to the bone at the first knuckle when the spring sprung. He might need stitches, but for now, three big Band-Aids and an ice-pack would do. The kids and Jeanne sat in the booth at the BP station across from the marina to stay out of the rain. Three hours and $150 later, the marina mechanic had the engine reassembled and running and the family motored out onto Geneva Lake, Ron's hand throbbing.

Ron cut the engine and called Emily to show her how to untie the mainsheet lashing the mainsail to the boom. A motorboat roared by, leaving a long coiling wake and jarring the little sailboat side to side and up and down. Ron shouted to everyone to get out of the way of the wildly swinging boom and gave the power-boater the finger with his healthy hand.

Sam tried to catch his puke in his new gloves, but breakfast sausage blew threw his fingers, covered his chest and speckled the starboard cockpit. Emily recoiled toward the opposite rail.

Jeanne scowled. Twenty minutes later, mainsail drawing, the boat started to move and heeled over. Emily screeched. Sam vomited again and tried not to cry, without success. Jeanne held onto the strap of Sam's life jacket so that he would not launch himself into the lake.

Ron wanted to unfurl the jib to add sail area (sail area is the equivalent of horsepower on a sailboat) to go faster, but Jeanne said no, absolutely. The kid's fingers and lips were shivering and blue and she was barely holding back her own awful gas-station brunch. Thirty minutes later, they clunked back into the dock — where the boat remained tied until August, when Ron's younger brother and his college buddy came to town.

Ron took another day off work, and the boys had a wild shirtless day drinking rum and blast-reaching across the lake. Great fun, until he sobered to a $350 dollar ticket for drinking while boating from the dock-cop, a blistering sunburn, and a spouse tired of taxiing kids in his absence.

Maybe not worth it, he thought.

They tried again the next summer, but the following spring the boat sat in the yard posted "$5,000 OBO," threadbare mainsail lashed to the boom. Ron told a work colleague at the next sales meeting that the family would try chartering when the kids got older.

Ron believes in his gut that sailing might be more fun than other things the family might do with its time together. He vividly recalls real wonder and exhilaration soloing a Penguin dinghy at Camp Kimonhon on Lake Olson. He has a shelf of sailing books, follows the America's Cup when it is run, and subscribes to numerous around-the-world race websites.

Jeanne and the kids are distracted by life. Sailing, for them, isn't life, but just one potential hobby amongst at least a dozen others. And, as far as they can tell, one that is very uncomfortable, expensive and scary. Ron's chance to show otherwise has passed.

If you ask would-be sailors what prevents them from sailing, almost half will admit that they don't know how to start. For those that decide to try on their own, about half do as Ron did, plunging in headfirst, alone and mostly on instinct. After they run into troubles, they stay on the periphery of the activity looking in, wishing they had either done it differently, earlier, or perhaps not at all.

Today in the U.S., more people have owned a sailboat sometime in their life than actively sail on one today.

CHAPTER 3

Making Time or Buying Time

In our short lives, we make many small decisions and a few big ones, the biggest being about how we spend our tiny allotment of time.

L ET'S DEEPEN OUR EXPLORATION of the pastime by distinguishing between time choices and time charters. A time choice is a slice of time that we take into our own hands, that we give shape to. It is time that we make. We own our choices. They might be deeply rooted or wafer-thin superficial, but they are ours nonetheless.

Time charters, on the other hand, are made for us by others. I don't mean as in a sailboat charter, per se, although that is part of this larger concept. I mean a charter as a general way of describing a thing that we consume, subscribe to, and are entertained by — a concession or an allotment where time is the product. A charter is time that we buy.

For example, when two or three people spontaneously agree that today is a good day for a walk with dogs, they've made a clear choice: a commitment to invest in time, talk, and shared decisions, whatever the outcome. They make a path into space and time, and invest something in a set of actions that shape the world in a way that it would not have been had they not decided to take that walk.

When the same three people go to a movie, they've subscribed to or chartered two or three hours of entertainment. They will get what they are given. The experience will occur within a prescribed set of outcomes that will be pretty much the same for all of them. The one decision they might make within that period is deciding not to stay through the show.

Of course, the walk or the movie can both be enjoyable, and the movie can feel energizing if it is good. But only the walk can return social benefits to the three who take it — like, for example, better insights into the minds of friends.

Unlike choices, we don't own our charters, so unmet expectations are someone else's fault, like disappointment at the operator who cuts short the merry-go-round at the county fair, or the realization that the movie-trailer assembled all the funniest parts into five minutes and that the full ninety wasn't worth the price of admission.

On the other hand, if a time choice doesn't meet expectations, it becomes something for us to examine in ourselves. It becomes a lesson.

The epitome of the charter is a visit to a theme park. Guests have an experience that is highly programmed, from the so-called adventure rides to the carefully arranged gift shops to the interactions with professional park staff who have been methodically trained in what to say and how to act. The result is a shrink-wrapped experience, and we know it.

Charters preordain our positive experiences. I cry like a baby every time I see *Forrest Gump,* but I am supposed to cry. It is what Tom Hanks, screenwriter Eric Roth and novelist Winston Groom intended. Don't get me wrong; I love the movie and will probably see it repeatedly. The charter isn't all bad, it's just not ours.

In contrast, if a choice delivers a positive experience, it becomes a source of pride and personal and community growth.

In this book, we will explore and understand our time choices — both large, hard ones and small, easy ones — to distinguish them from charters, to see how they matter.

Is it naive, cold or a bit ostentatious to suggest that a

pastime deserves choosing at all (let alone a book about it) at a time when people may be hungry and jobs may be hard to hold? The key point is that anyone that edges even a short inch over the economic threshold that we call subsistence has a certain amount of time to use as they wish. That is what life is: time, subject to choices about how it will be spent. This book suggests that one measure of the health of a society is how its people collectively use their spare stretches of it, to the benefit of individuals, families, and communities as a whole. I will not, however, suggest or imply that games or hobbies can create food or safety. They can't.

Furthermore, it would be a cop-out to write a book that glorifies the way things used to be, suggesting that the way it is now is somehow weaker or diminished or is someone else's fault. This is not going to be about how today's youth are more easily distracted or lazy. Nor does it suggest that they are somehow made different by Facebook and the Wii. They are not.

It is not what we choose to do, but how we go about doing it that determines its value. I will propose, simply, that our health and happiness are rooted in the interactions that we have with each other, and that these interactions are wholly in our control.

The best are chosen. The rest are charters.

CHAPTER 4

Danny Learns to Sail

Like most kids, Danny's attraction is to things that are more fun. So sailing passes muster . . . for now.

ANNY'S PARENTS ARE BOTH dentists. They own a powerboat but do not use it much. In the 1990s, Danny's dad wanted to fish and his mom wanted to sunbathe. The boat they chose was an unsatisfactory compromise that did not do either well.

But before they could sell it, Danny caught the sailing bug at the local yacht club near their dock in the municipal marina. So the family kept the boat and the membership, and Danny's parents became summer-season cabbies, dropping Danny at the club gates for sailing lessons four times a week.

Danny's sailing development took the routine path of a Millennial Generation sailor.

First he learned the basics of rigging, launching, boarding, the points of sail and safety on a trainer called a Designer's Choice (DC). He learned to capsize and recover gracefully by righting an overturned boat. He graduated to his own Optimist[7], or "Opti," and then to the two-person International 420[8]. By the time Danny was sixteen, he was big enough to sail against the local college team on his own Laser[9], and he was making eleven bucks an hour teaching nine-year-olds on the DCs.

Danny won the club youth championship three years in a row and crewed on various member-owned boats including Solings, Lightnings, J-105s and an assortment of the bigger, faster handicap racers. By the time Danny was ready for college he had sailed in a half-dozen overnight distance races and twenty regattas, and he had started and finished hundreds of course races.

----

7 An Optimist is an 8-foot-long dinghy, designed to be sailed alone by a child aged 8 to 15 years old. 140,000 boats are registered in the one-design fleet.

8 An International 420 is a 13-foot planing dinghy designed in France as a two-person trainer.

9 A Laser is a popular and powerful single-handed dinghy designed by Bruce Kirby in the late 1960s and still in production today.

Danny is an accomplished racing sailor. He can trim any sail very well, and he is light on his feet, quick to solve problems and is a talented driver.

Danny's senses are tuned to speed. When the boat is well balanced he holds the tiller with a light touch, subtly sculling to nudge the bow around the next wave and down and to prevent slapping, slamming or rocking that would eat boat speed. Danny's eyes scan the waves four boat lengths ahead and the performance instruments four feet from where he sits.

From the wind angle, direction and speed data, he computes the factors that affect acceleration and deceleration in his head. He sets private speed goals and when he hits them, he sets higher goals again. Once he has achieved what he thinks is the maximum speed, he shifts gears and works toward the longest period of sustained top speed. Danny would drive for hours and only break for food or drink, and maybe not then.

Unfortunately, as good as he is, according to known participation trends, there is a high probability that Danny will not be a sailor much longer, in large part because he doesn't associate sailing with the things that he assumes will be important soon in his life, like a career, and perhaps a wife and kids. As soon as Danny graduates from college, he will find something that means more to him, and sailing will be one of the programs, one of the things he tried and mastered as a kid.

It is only in the last twenty years that sailing has become one option in an array of sophisticated, optional, highly-organized kids-only summer programs.

Like its soccer, dance, and baseball brethren, the sailing program teaches skills and gamesmanship very well. Even as overall participation in sailing is way down, the overall level of sailboat racing skill in the U.S. has perhaps never been greater then now. Youth sailing programs teach the fundamental skills required to sail a boat first, and then, to hold the attention of their participants, focus on skills repetition and the rules and techniques used to race a boat around buoys against other kids. After basic skills are secure, the kids usually sail alone in small boats.

So for as much pure entertainment as Danny derives from sailing, his reward comes primarily from the little burst of adrenaline that he receives when he tacks or jibes well, or when he passes a fellow classmate on a racing leg. He's not there for social reasons or to connect with something larger, he's there because it is as good as any other summer program choice and he likes to beat the other kids in races.

Like soccer, dance and baseball, sailing programs have become the source of intense competitive pressure, both across programs and within them, but not only the kind one might think. Programs pit kids against each other in competition for trophies, and they also create competition for time within kids. A kid may try sailing, realize that it is a large commitment and move onto the next craft or instrument or sport. Or a teen who might want to sail but didn't start early may find that he or she is too far behind to ever catch up with kids like Danny, and determine it a waste of time to try.

Youth programs create a third dimension of competition: that for the time of the child within the family. More than one mother told me that she doesn't see her son anymore, except when taxiing or waving from far away, and she misses his company. She's proud of his skills, but doesn't understand them and doesn't see how they will matter in his future.

If you care about culture this may make you sad; or you might chalk it up to the natural cycles of human and economic development. We all seem to be moving faster and doing more. Why shouldn't kids?

Stepping back to a time before kids-only programs, we can see that while we initially might have chosen to fish, sail, sew, ride horses or hunt for fun, the practice descends directly from an earlier economic setting when it was work, not play. As work, it carried honor and reward. My Papou's memories were not of recreational craft or racing sailboats, but of cargo-carrying and work boats with Greek sailors and fishermen and women harvesting the sea or delivering goods for a living.

As technology and economies develop, the motivation to fish, weave, hunt, sew, or sail shifts from economic to nostalgic. People who make quilts honor the skills of their quilt-making grandparents. People who raise horses think back to the brave riders in the old West, soldier heroes on horseback, or to great grandparents who farmed. People who play classical music immerse themselves in it, mirroring the shapes and styles of the masters.

Until recently, sailing was like many other pastimes of the mid–20th century: a way to be nostalgic, to carry on a tradition, to honor the skills of grandparents and great-parents who sailed, likely as laborers, perhaps as soldiers. But we did it in a social sporting environment in their honor. Sailing had the feeling of a spontaneous burst of fun infused with reflection, like a Frisbee game at a family reunion. Everyone left both physically and emotionally satisfied.

When an activity crosses over the bridge from necessity to nicety, however, its long-term growth prospects depend upon whether the emotional thread is able to strengthen in new ways or not.

In summary, first an activity is work, then it adds play as it continues to honor work. Then, as the traditional aspects start to fade, it must find something else that is as powerful as honor, or else it starts to lose its impact and therefore its staying power.

Eventually our motivation to do such things is diluted to a vague desire to be entertained, in the face of so many other popular entertainment options. Sometimes we try to hold on for a time by developing kids-only programs (often called outreach programs) to provide the entertainment, and then we wonder why young adults leave and don't return.

It is easy to conclude that for pastimes that are declining, the social and emotional threads have weakened, risking the activities to the fate of the merely curious, or to the people like Danny who seek one last win before they grow up and get serious about something that matters.

CHAPTER 5

Why Did We Start Sailing?

Every free time activity has someone who lights the match — the person(s) who defines the activity for its enthusiastic early-adopters, or redefines it to make it seem accessible. Fly fishing has Hemingway. Hunting has Teddy Roosevelt. Jazz has Coltrane. Sailing has the Kennedys.

HOME AFTER FIGHTING IN the European or Pacific theaters, and without much in the way of financial means, the World War II generation went to school on the GI bill, starting in the mid-1940s. Having looked into the eyes of evil, and flush with fresh higher education, Americans generally recognized the privilege of time on this planet and were motivated to use the balance of theirs well. They studied to make contributions as engineers, teachers and entrepreneurs, setting up the greatest productivity and prosperity explosion ever.

By the 1960s, they were the largest, most prosperous and most influential middle class in human history, responsible for building more industry, commerce, public infrastructure and valued social institutions like schools, parks and hospitals than had ever been amassed before. They, together with their 2.6 kids, reinvented the pastime.

Before the war, sandlot baseball and a night by the cabinet radio dominated much of American free time. Before the war, fathers and sons might step outside to play a bit of catch. Mothers and daughters gardened or sewed or embroidered. Before the war, one might consider the hard work of rigging and launching a boat to be the lot of working-class Maine fisherfolk — or the sailing of a yacht to be the provenance of the few idle rich.

From the mid-1950s into the 1970s, America was proud, prosperous, powerful and generally staunchly populist. We often think of the 1960s as a time only of cultural and political wars, but it was also a time of stable wages, lower costs of living, energy and therefore, improving quality of life. JFK's example of heroism, and his ideas of service, innovation and strength came of age, and we went with him. My dad had his ties and slacks. My mom had her hair. (They still do.)

Images of young John F. and Jackie Kennedy sailing off Cape Code appeared in *Time* magazine and many other publications starting in about 1953. These images may be partly responsible for launching sailing as a popular pastime, and still influence what sailing means to many American sailors today.

In the pictures, Jack and Jackie can be seen in casual sun clothes, rigging and sailing small sailboats off sandy beaches. The images drip romance, in-the-moment joy and freedom. While we expect the Kennedys to go on to greatness, as they would, these images tell us that sailing is accessible and modest, but core and formative to our relationships and our potential as partners, leaders and citizens. The handsome couple in those boats looks like they are making memories, and they are doing it under sail power.

Once we've been introduced to an idea, it takes a growing core group of participants and simple, basic economic and social factors to give it critical mass, to advance its popularity to the point that it becomes part of the social lubricant that defines culture. Sailing soon found an audience of World War II vets and their kids, who together embraced sailing in full force.

In the mid-1950s, about a decade after the war, roughly the time when the Kennedy sailing pictures first appeared, those first children of the veterans were about ten years old.

It is no coincidence that this is when impromptu and then organized sailing took off. Fleets of sailboats popped up on bays and lakes all over America.

By 1964, the Snipe fleet on Lake Springfield, a reservoir surrounded by cornfields in central Illinois, boasted more than 50 boats.

In 1974, the National Championship was held at Lake Springfield, and hundreds sailed. Carl Alberg's Ensign, a 22-foot, deep-keeled boat for day sailing and racing, found 1,600 customers. Fleets of designs like Lightnings, Flying Dutchmen, Cat boats, scows, and Hobie cats became the weekend platforms and the larger social communities for dads and sons all over the country. (Those same sons are the men who dominate sailing today.)

By the late 1980s, almost ten million middle-class Americans called themselves active sailors, spending an average of five days (120 hours) a year on the water[10].

Sailing was indeed part of our social fabric.

---

10 Gartner, William C., and Lime, David W., *Trends in Outdoor Recreation, Leisure and Tourism.* CABI Publishing, 2000.

NICHOLAS D. HAYES

CHAPTER 6

Communities of Interest

*To make the economics work for more people than just the
adventurers or the wealthy, we needed shared infrastructure
and some technology.*

O NE SUMMER SATURDAY IN the mid-1980s, I lowered
my head and walked past the "members-only" sign
and through the tall gate at one of the local yacht
clubs, wondering if I would be in trouble for doing so. I
fully expected to be strong-armed back to the parking lot
but nobody seemed to notice me.

The week before, a friend of a friend had invited my
wife and me to ride along on his cruising sailboat to take
pictures at the start of the Queen's Cup, an overnight race
across Lake Michigan. Two hundred boats lined up in
groups and pointed their bows eastward into the dark as

the sun set behind them. It looked cold, dangerous and foreign, but I wanted in.

That night I accepted an invitation from the skipper to try my hand as foredeck crew on his other boat, a three-person racing keelboat called a Soling.

Since that Saturday morning twenty-five years ago, no less than 80% of my summer Saturday mornings have begun at a yacht club, getting ready to go sailing or racing for the day or for the weekend or summer vacation.

Sailing & Yacht Clubs

About 20% of American sailors, roughly 365,000 people, are members of some sort of yacht or boat club. When you add others who pass through these places en route to a ride on a boat, like the crew and the family and friends of the sailboat owner, yacht clubs touch about 70% of all American sailors. This is especially true for sailors who choose to race. Of sailboat owners who race their boats, 80% are club members, since clubs are the de facto local organizing body of the sport.

Yacht club lore is rich with tales of vast wealth, power and elitism, some of it accurate, but most of it greatly exaggerated and some of it patently untrue. To understand how and why sailing grew and is struggling now, it is important to deconstruct the dusty myths about yachts and yacht clubs and reconstruct what was behind the early development of sailing as a pastime and sailing clubs in the United States that made it popular.

Club bylaws tell who, how, when and why a club was formed. Reviewing these records, one finds three basic club types.

A handful of yacht clubs were formed during the Gilded Age by industrial magnates like Carnegie and Vanderbilt. These titans agreed to gather privately near and on the water, not just because they liked their yachts, but because shipping and boat building were among the chief *business interests* of the members. These were exclusive business organizations where men in powerful positions gathered to share secrets and trade. They formed not as communities of sailors, but instead with missions to further naval architecture and boat building during the peak years of an industrial revolution that was transforming developed nations in the Americas and Europe. Water-born shipment of raw materials and consumer goods was exploding, and speed meant advantage.

Clubs also became centers of high-stakes gaming because the members felt that competition might drive technological advancement. The first America's Cup race was won in 1851 by a founding member of the New York Yacht Club, John Cox Stevens, to mark his wager that his pleasure yacht *America* was faster than Great Britain's Royal Yacht Squadron. And it was.

Most sailing historians hold the first America's Cup race to be straightforward upper-crust gamesmanship. In reality, Steven's vessel may well have been a platform for promoting the advantages of an evolving hull with a notably fine bow and broad, shallow stern. Supremacy in sailing technology was extremely important to the commercial interests of the time. The success of *America* was part of the same drive for speed and innovation as the American clipper ships that had come by the mid-1800s to dominate global shipping lanes, leading to great economic advantage. By winning his challenge, Stevens helped to drive home the point that the U.S. could triumph in a high-stakes game, for those who wondered who had the best sailing technology of the time. The United States was well on its way to becoming a world power by virtue of its skills on the high seas, and of course this power resulted in new American wealth.

Another 20% of yacht clubs popped up in the period between the turn of the century and into the early 1930s, in mostly large affluent industrial cities on the water, intent on imitating the elite clubs of the East. Unfortunately, in the late 1930s, many Americans struggled to feed their families, and a pastime like sailing was simply out of the question.

One might easily conclude that even today, yacht clubs

face an image problem resulting from the public display of wealth just behind the tall, iron gates that were erected around some of those clubs during the Depression. Then came the war, and clubs stopped forming for a while.

In reality, only a handful of yacht clubs can or should claim such entrepreneurial or elitist pedigree. Four in five of the oldest clubs and all younger clubs report far more modest beginnings. For example, the Annapolis Yacht Club, which anchors a large and vibrant sailing community today, was formed by four guys who liked to canoe on the Chesapeake.

Indeed, the vast majority of yacht clubs in the U.S. opened as a populist answer to the demand for sailing expressed by groups within a growing, educated pre-boomer and boomer middle-class between 1949 and 1979. Most clubs were formed by teachers, engineers and salespeople like Vince and Larry, so that they could pool resources to go sailing.

They were more like member-owned and managed cooperatives than centers of high society or financial power. By their charter, clubs simply spread the high cost of storage, access to the water by way of the valuable land near it, event management and sometimes insurance among a group of people with a common interest: being on the water in their spare time.

Starting in the 1970s, many clubs began to widen their focus to stay in step with their members. Most created training programs for members' children or, in some cases, for the general population. Some built and rented boat-slips and moorings. Most organized races between members. Many created special annual racing events and invited others from out of town. Some diversified by welcoming power-boaters. Some had a power-boat orientation from the start.

Some of the clubs organized winter outdoor programs like skiing. Some added food and drink services, and some added retail boutiques. Some constructed swimming pools, tennis courts and health centers. Some offered combined memberships with golf clubs.

Many of today's yacht clubs face a tough challenge. They often maintain very expensive infrastructure (80% of U.S. clubs operate a year-round clubhouse with a bar and restaurant) on valuable waterfront land. They have hired staffs and created services to support the changing needs of one age group. But the next age group is smaller in number and doesn't appear as interested in what those clubs have to offer.

Member growth and program participation are the top two challenges faced by clubs,[11] obviously an outcome of an aging membership that would rather eat and visit than sail or race. It is not an exaggeration to say that today, club members are dying faster than new ones are joining. Simple demographics and economics say that we will have fewer yacht clubs in the United States, and very soon.

But it isn't just demographics. Many have simply lost their way, forgetting the core idea that they are there to make it possible to choose to sail. The vast majority of yacht clubs in the U.S. were formed to make sailing popular by making it accessible. Not easy, because it isn't. Just within reach.

Some still do, and many still can.

Surprisingly, the median cost of membership in all yacht clubs in the United States is still only about $50 a month, comparable to or less than the price paid for cable television or cell-phone service by tens of millions of American households at all economic levels.[12] Of course, clubs that have lavishly overbuilt and lost their focus on sailing are usually clubs that cost much more.

Still, many clubs remain surprisingly affordable and some are downright cheap. Depending on where you live, member dues at a nearby club might be as little as twenty dollars a month or even just fifty dollars a year. Some clubs

....

11 U.S. Sailing. "2007 Study of Yacht Clubs."

12 Ibid.

even offer their members access to a fleet of boats to use as they wish.

One might then wonder why clubs can't recruit members at the same pace that they lose them? Most often, it turns out that member recruitment is not about the money. Successful clubs understand that it is about the time. Strong clubs create a kind of time bank, where time invested returns interest. So members contribute spare time and get better time back.

James Buchanan's 1965 article "The Economic Theory of Clubs" explains that clubs are tools to contain cost and time. He wrote that an important means of reducing costs (thereby extending access) is to enter into cost-sharing agreements. Since time is a cost, it makes sense that this concept also applies to time. We might say that an important means of extending time is to enter into time-sharing agreements. This simple idea is what strong clubs do.

If you would measure a club's well-being by the number of family generations that congregate there, it is easy to see that today's healthy clubs are still the populist ones. They avoid hiring professionals when they can and instead insist that members volunteer to help with dock and grounds upkeep, services and programming. To keep carrying costs low, they reject expensive projects. These clubs sidestep the charter — the paid program — seeing it as a way of diluting the value of the membership, no matter the fees. Instead, they call on members to build self-propagating sailing activities that hold to the same principles of volunteerism and pooled resources and time that the founders envisioned.

The healthiest clubs recognize that as organizations they depend completely on the voluntary time choice. They exist to facilitate the harder choices, allowing diverse groups to come together for activities more difficult or costly to do separately. As a result, they become institutions of loyalty and longevity.

When clubs insist that members give of their time in order be members, they develop a sustainable vitality rooted in the commitments made in relationships between the people in them. Of course, this makes it harder for some, but it makes it much better for those that enlist.

The clubs that stay together do so because a small group of people share a common interest and agree to cooperate to promote and protect that interest by giving up some of their time. It is not unlike a family, a tribe, or a subculture. Like these other small human communities, healthy clubs are those that have found the formula for multi-generational cooperation, which, in turn, provides the fertile ground for mentoring.

Sailboat Technology

Since teachers, salespeople and other professionals with modest incomes could not afford yachts, they bought boats that they could afford. To understand the early days of the development of sailing, we must return to World War II as the source of technological innovation, which in turn made sailing far less expensive.

In 1942, the company Owens Corning was saturating fibers of glass in a polyester resin to turn out light but strong parts for fighter airplanes. The material was easy and fast to work with and the parts were highly durable. When the war was over, the race to find commercial applications for fiberglass construction began. It didn't take long. By 1947, fiberglass sailboats manufactured by General Electric were on display at boat shows around the country.

Before fiberglass, most boats were made of wood or steel, materials that constantly break down. The time and expense required to keep a wooden or a steel boat fresh and seaworthy was and still is too high for someone who does not make a living from it or who only has weekends or evenings to commit to it. Fiberglass made sailing safer, too. Fiberglass boats didn't leak and could withstand incredible punishment.

Fiberglass boats can start out affordable and often hold their value. Many boats built in the 1950s remain seaworthy and useful today. Imagine buying a car built in 1950 for practical, safe transportation in 2009. Fiberglass does this for sailboats.

For the boat designer, fiberglass allowed anyone with an idea about what makes a good boat to have their design put into production and tested against other ideas. Since the fiberglass sailboat hit the market fifty years ago, hundreds of hull designs have gone into production, and thousands more prototypes have been fashioned by artisans, holding the interest of upgrading boomers.

Recently, sailboat makers and their engineers have computerized much of the building process, and they are now making the most uniform and efficient sailboats ever.

Driven by the highest end of racing competition, new materials and construction processes come to sailing every year and some spin out to other markets. Many racing sails are made of Mylar, Kevlar and carbon fiber. At the highest end of the sport, titanium is used in key parts like shackles. Wireless computers and complex electronic sensors cover many boats. Honeycombed and lightweight foam plastics are used in hull cores. But the basic building block of resin-encapsulated glass fibers remains unchanged since the end of World War II.

So since World War II, clubs and fiberglass have come together to make sailing possible. Today, due to shared costs and smart technology, sailing remains a most affordable pastime. At any moment, in any city near water, one can find a dusty but serviceable, trailer-launched fiberglass boat large enough to sleep and feed a family of four, with a motor, trailer, sails, safety equipment and line for a couple thousand dollars. The same boat with a new coat of paint and new cushion covers might sell for six or seven thousand dollars.

In some cities, these long-living fiberglass sailboats have been donated to form public fleets run by not-for-profit community sailing centers. These centers use those serviceable vessels as training platforms for underprivileged kids or as shared fleets for adults who lack the means to buy their own boats.

A sailor seeking greater adventure might consider investing in a used 30-foot sailboat with headroom, beds for four, a diesel engine, sails, a galley, a head and instruments for less than a used Volkswagen Passat with 50,000 miles. He or she could moor the boat for somewhere between $30 and $300 a month. (Slips usually cost much more.) For all practical purposes, such a boat might carry passengers all over the world and, when it returns, be worth about the same amount as when it started.

A sailor with racing ambitions can join a club, gather some members and friends and enter the very same 30-footer in a race and be scored on a handicap. He or she might choose instead to join a club fleet of small identical racers, with boats ranging in price from hundreds to a few thousands of dollars.

Of course, one with greater financial means might choose to create his or her own club and racing syndicate, locate it on prime French Riviera real estate and spend upwards of three hundred million for their own America's Cup campaign. Like the ten or twelve violinists who hold and play a Stradivarius, these are the rare exceptions in sailing, not the norm.

The hidden fact is that, measured in dollars and time, sailing can be a relatively inexpensive pastime choice. Depending on where one lives, and on one's sailing aspirations, active engagement in sailing might cost somewhere between cable TV and a small car payment. Of course, it can cost much more, but it doesn't have to. Even in its least expensive forms, sailing is sure to return far finer rewards than the TV or the car. It's also true, according to measures of sailor enthusiasm, that low-cost sailing yields as much enjoyment as high-cost sailing.

Inexpensvie sailing most often happens in clubs, coops and consortiums. For the participants who take advantage of those opportunities, cost is often not the main barrier to popularity.

In summary, sailing clubs and fiberglass sailboats are valuable to us not because they are exclusive, expensive or rare, but because they deliver social value over long periods. Sailing is not yachting, though many outside the pastime mistake it for that, and sailing is by no means just for the privileged, although nearly every sailor will say that it is a privilege. The difference is clear.

Sailing is closer to fishing or sewing or singing in a group — a special time that happens when some people choose to invest in each other.

CHAPTER 7

T.J. Finds a Career in Sailing

Who doesn't dream of making a career out of their life's passion? Isn't that what we all want?

VINCE RETURNED TO CHARLESTON from Korea and took a sales job with a small insurance company. He had been a solid salesperson but he was a better manager, so after a few years in the field he was promoted to regional manager and was brought into the corporate office. Seven years and three promotions later he was the Senior Vice President of Sales. On nights and weekends, he and his wife Calayag and son T.J. (short for Tubig James) went sailing.

The family boat was a Tartan 30, a fiberglass sloop with room for four or five. They would enter it in a race a couple of times a year and would cruise up and down the intercoastal waterway at least five weekends a summer. Calayag would cover T.J. in wool sweaters, a rain slicker and a big orange lifejacket, and he would shed them all to climb the mainsheet and swing from the boom like Tarzan.

When he was tired, the boy would curl into his mother's lap in the cockpit and listen to stories of the finest places on earth, all reachable only by boat, she said. She told him about the Philippine Islands of her childhood, and about when she first gazed on the Golden Gate Bridge from the ship when they came to America. His favorite story was of the bay marked by the Toledo Harbor Light where, according to Calayag, the waves could be square not smooth and the water was always sweet not salty.

Then, when T.J. was seven, his mother Calayag died of ovarian cancer. The boat was put away for a few years.

When T.J. was thirteen, Vince married his secretary Cynthia, who didn't sail, and bought a secondhand Star class open-cockpit racing sailboat so that he and his son could be a team. They won the club fleet championship the second season with the boat. In the next few spectacular summers, father and son collected a closet full of trophies, flags and stories.

Vince collapsed and died at a conference in Daytona Beach of a massive heart-attack at the age of 54, leaving T.J.

with the Star, no blood relative, $50,000 of life insurance for college and a hole in his heart.

The Tartan was sold to pay down the home mortgage, so that T.J. and his stepmother Cynthia would not have to worry about a roof. However, neither T.J. nor Cynthia wanted to be under the same one.

T.J. moved in with his buddy Ken and chose technical school over college so that he could learn to fix his Dodge Charger. By the time he was twenty-two the college fund was nearly gone, T.J. had dropped out of school twice, and the Charger was on top of blocks in Ken's back yard. But the Star was still on top of the club fleet. T.J. was unbeatable. He could grab two kids out of the junior program, fly ten-year-old sails, and still put a leg on the nearest competitor.

For T.J., sailing was cathartic. He could succeed at something difficult with the ease of an artist. His troubles seemed to vanish on the water, so he spent as much time there as he could. Everyone around him knew it.

Dick Bavell, the wealthy president of the insurance company where Vince had worked, bought a two-year-old IMS 50 that had been used as a training platform for a defunct America's Cup syndicate, and had plans to campaign it. Bavel named it *Rolero* (a play on Ravel's *Bolero,* made famous by Bo Derek in the movie *10*). T.J. was his first choice to be on the foredeck because he was big, strong and light on his feet.

Since T.J. needed to earn some money to be able to sail, Dick hired him to care for the boat. T.J. scrubbed the deck, polished the brightwork, inspected and replaced rigging, mended the sails and changed the engine oil. T.J. moved out of Ken's place and into the aft cabin of the boat and showered at the marina and ate dinner at the bar.

Dick campaigned *Rolero* vigorously up and down the East coast, entering it wherever a few more 50-footers were sailing. They did the Block Island Race Week, the Newport to Bermuda Race, the Southern Ocean Racing Circuit and the Miami to Nassau race, among many others.

T.J. was also in charge of getting the boat to the places that Dick needed it to be. By the time he was twenty-five years old, T.J. had raced in one hundred major events and sailed over ten thousand miles. He had experienced two hurricanes, learned celestial and electronic navigation and sailmaking, and was a qualified and artful rigger. He had been promoted from the foredeck to mainsail trimmer, and *Rolero* became *Rolero II* when Dick's options matured and he sold the original for a newer, faster Swan 60.

T.J. had found his place. Sailing was not a pastime; it was a living. He had sailed to, from and in exotic locations all over the world. He had met and sailed with acquaintances from Harvard, Oxford and Wall Street, in Indonesia, South Africa, and the Olympics.

After about ten years, Dick tired of the big bills and time associated with an ocean racing campaign and moved on to hedge funds. The boat was bought by a Spaniard and sent to the Mediterranean. T.J. was without a job and a place to live. He took odd jobs for a while and looked for other boat owners who might hire a boat manager. Every other spring he would land such a job and every other fall it would dry up. Finally he found himself doing odd jobs repairing fiberglass and spraying paint.

He tried to settle. He married for a while, but when she wanted kids, he had to argue against the idea. He could never be sure where or if he would be working. So it didn't last.

Every activity has its professionals. This per se is not a bad thing. Pros set the performance standard and can inspire others to new levels of effort or achievement. However, the organic vitality of an activity can be measured by a ratio of amateurs to professionals active in it, since the amateurs fund the pros either directly, as with Dick and T.J., or indirectly via sponsorships, branding and other commissions. When too many pros tax too few amateurs, some amateurs will start to wonder why they are in it. "He's getting paid for something I have to spend to do."

In 2008, no less than 5% of all sailors were pros in some fashion: paid to sail or fix boats or sell something related to sailing. Compare sailing to music, where only one in 300 people who play are paid for it; or soccer, where only one in 1,000 are economically linked.

But the issue is larger than just one of financing the pro's fun. The existence of people who buy and sell pastimes is a strong indication that the activity is becoming a curiosity. It means that devotion among amateurs is eroding. It is not far, metaphorically, from the wave machine at an indoor water park. Ten bucks for fifteen minutes of bitchin', chartered fun, so to speak.

The issue is one of asymmetrical commitment. The wave-machine operator may be a world-class surfer trying desperately to remain connected in any way possible, but the wave rider usually finds it interesting if only for a few minutes. Asymmetrical commitment is the sad socioeconomic consequence of the charter. It turns the pastime into a crutch for some and a whim for everyone else.

T.J. could not survive without sailing, while Dick could take it or leave it. Any shift in Dick's preferences, for whatever reason, puts T.J. at huge risk. Likewise, if kids stop wanting to ride the wave machine, attendants will have to find something else to do than surf.

T.J., meanwhile, loves sailing, but cannot easily share it freely because it is not in his economic interest. He must get paid to sail. Out of financial necessity, T.J. keeps a careful throttle on what he shares and what he protects as his trade knowledge, or he runs the risk of eroding his market value as a professional.

Then, when Dick moves on and T.J. is forced to move on because he has aged out or there are not any more *Roleros,* all that is left is a stack of payroll stubs, some dusty trophies and memories of Vince, and a vague but warm sense that Calayag wished that her son had kept on his lifejacket.

CHAPTER 8

Larry, Sailing Alone

Larry has owned three sailboats, each more expensive and suited to his evolving needs than the last.

L ARRY WAS AN ARCHITECT by trade and teaches design at a local college to fill some of his time in retirement. His first boat was a used Paceship 28, bought as a family toy when his kids were young.

Larry's wife Phyllis never took to sailing. Their three kids would opt in a half-dozen times a summer. And every July 4th, the whole family would spend the day on the water, sailing, swimming and then watching fireworks from the deck. For a time, Larry ran a sort of open sail night for his office mates. He'd supply the boat on Thursday nights, and the single guys from work would bring beer and sandwiches.

The Paceship was cheap — less than an old used car — but ugly, clumsy and slow, so when he could afford it, Larry upgraded to a roomier, sleeker and more powerful Catalina 30, thinking it would be a more attractive platform for the family. Phyllis was still not interested and the kids went to college. The guys from the office got married and found other things to do.

Larry was left to either not sail or learn to sail the bigger boat alone. He added new systems like a roller furling headsail and lazy jacks on the mainsail to make the boat more manageable, but it was still a bit too large for just one person, especially when docking. When his former employer offered to buy his stock options, he jumped, and found himself with a modest windfall. He traded up to a smaller but brand-new Alerion 28, even easier to sail alone, but still comfortable for visiting kids and grandkids.

Every spring I get a call from Larry to talk about my plans and his, about launch schedules and vacation ideas and the latest upgrades to improve the experience. He complains about his trouble motivating family and friends. I complain that the number of boats racing on the bay is on the decline. And we agree that we will sail together, which we almost never do.

One Saturday I came off the race course and Larry was walking down the dock with a sandwich cooler and an extra sweatshirt. Of course he invited me to join him for a couple of hours and, on this day, I had no commitments, so I did.

We motored past the breakwater and out onto the lake where we unfurled the sails and cruised southeast on a reach for an hour. I had just finished three hours of racing, with the constant crew dialogue needed to tune and adjust every line and sail to find the highest boat speed. Larry and I just lumbered along. If the sails were over- or under-trimmed, he didn't move them, he made rough course corrections. If the boat slowed, we waited until it started moving again.

I complied for a while, but finally unable to keep myself from seeking speed, I jumped forward to kick to unstick and then readjust the location of a jib car. The boat responded, feeling more balanced, easier to steer, and just a bit faster.

Larry, a 35-year veteran, eyebrows raised and wondering, asked what I had just done. He had never before moved the jib car and didn't understand its purpose.

If you ask a self-described sailor what they intend to do with their next boat or why they bought the boat that they own, most will tell you that they planned to go day sailing. Day sailing is the simplest way to sail. As long as you have access to a boat, you climb on, raise sails and go for a ride. You start and finish in the same place. For all practical purposes, it is the entry point to the rest of the pastime.

In Larry's case, it is all he ever does. Larry has simply sidestepped the problem of coordinating a group by gearing up to go day sailing alone.

That does not mean that Larry is any less avid than Danny or T.J. All told, including purchase, storage and care, Larry has committed upwards of 40% of his free time and 25% of his free cash and net worth to sailing over the last 35 years, even though he does not have a serious commitment from anyone in his family that it matters to them.

Larry works out the scheduling snags with his wife, then gets himself up on Saturday mornings, packs one tuna sandwich and two diet sodas, drives thirty minutes to the lake, muscles his four-ton boat out of tight quarters, and escapes to a different place. Larry has broken down many tall barriers to do what he does. He has made investments and complex arrangements to find the tools and the time. And he has developed enough confidence in his skills to leave shore alone.

Larry is a member of the largest group in American sailing. He is educated, male, retired, and has ample discretionary time and some spare cash. He wishes more people would go with him, but if they don't, he will go on his own.

He sails because, to him, his time on the water is time well spent. First he buries his fears, focuses his mind on complex tasks to solve problems and is sure that the process improves his life off the water. Given research that shows that an active mind and body are key to good health in late-life, Larry is right.

He also sails because it gives him the time to reflect.

Memory making was the young-adulthood and mid-life modus operandi of Americans born between 1935 and 1955. In between Woodstock and the fall of the Wall, Larry's generation invented backpacking and then trekked to the summit of Mount Everest, raced dirt bikes and then rode hogs to Sturgis, invented scuba and then swam with the whales off the Baja Peninsula, collected dinosaur fossils on volunteer digs in the desert to chart our past. Now it is boarding cruise-ships to the poles to catch a glimpse of the melting ice-pack to imagine our future.

Tapping their parents' post-war energy, boomers like Larry have consistently selected pastimes that shape an idealized view of themselves, their families and their role in the world. Throughout, they've assembled a life of memories.

Now, for the boomers, memory recovery — nostalgia for earlier ways, past adventures and the people that mattered along the way — is high on their agenda. On the water, Larry is transported backward in time when he sails. Larry's mental images might include an honorable struggle against nature and age as captured by Hemingway, or Conrad's bold, rough merchant mariner, or Shackleton's undaunted courage, or the superior strategic intellect of Commodore Perry, or simply the time he spent with his dad when he was twelve.

One boomer sailor told me, "The other day I caught myself thinking about my dad while sailing. He never sailed, not once in his life. We fished together when I was a kid. But he was still on my mind while I was on the water." For him, sailing provides a good place to recall.

People who earn their living in the sailing industry are pegged to good customers like Larry. The brokers, the builders, magazines, the yacht clubs and most gear-makers have stayed right with him, each step of the way. First, they made boats and gear that assumed that Larry would sail for social reasons. When his kids moved on, they switched over to make it as easy as possible for him to sail alone. All for good reason. There are not as many younger Americans, and they have less time and money than Larry.

Industry always tools to meet demand, it never shapes it. Larry doesn't want to sail alone most of the time, but because he does, industry is there to help. As a result, marinas up and down American coastlines are crowded with large, simple-to-sail boats, vessels that leave the dock with one, perhaps two late-year boomers a couple of times a month, or less often, and leave kids and grandkids at home.

CHAPTER 9

Lifelong Learning

Things worth a lifetime learning curve are things that perpetually challenge and amaze.

S AILING IS OFTEN EXPLAINED by lifelong sailors as lifelong learning. When you ask sailors about their level of experience, novices will often call themselves experts, even if they are unaware of and haven't passed key thresholds.

On the other hand, many who have sailed for years will astutely identify themselves as perpetual students of sailing, at least to their closest friends or in the privacy of an interview.

There is a bit of ego involved. Once you know a few of the funny names of the parts of a boat, you feel a bit special.

Then when you realize that they do much more than you thought, you're a bit humbled.

There are generally two stages in learning to sail. The first is the period of rough sketching, when a sailor recognizes energy in the wind, the relationship of a sail's orientation to the direction of the wind, and how a sailboat responds to coarse changes in either wind direction or velocity or boat direction. During this stage sailors share a general sense of wonder that a boat can sail within about forty-five degrees on an angle that is partially into the wind, amazement at the powerful sound of the bow slicing the waves in its way, and the thrill that moving at about six miles an hour can seem so fast and be so much fun.

Most people who try sailing and, arguably, many who have done it for years, never graduate from the first stage of rough sketching. For the most part they are content with that. After all, basic sailing skills can deliver us between two ports, across oceans or around the world. Much confidence is gained by the sailor who steers a boat safely from one place to another, whether in an hour or in a year, whether at eight or eighty years of age. Rough sketches can still be hung on the refrigerator door and they bring much pleasure.

The second learning stage is when the art is refined, when the science explains the art and the simple pencil marks are replaced with color, shade and dimension.

Here, a sailor begins to recognize and harness aerodynamics, hydrodynamics and mechanics, bound seamlessly with their scientific and mathematical cousins thermodynamics and physics. And on boats with teams, the savvy sailor applies a bit of sociology as glue.

The second-stage sailor sees a sail not as a tool to catch the wind, but as a machine to alter the course of the wind, a foil that creates lift which, when countered by lateral resistance from a keel or centerboard, multiplies the available energy in the wind. Here the sail begins to represent a series of shapes presented to the wind, almost infinitely flexible in the task of seeking peak efficiency while stealing power from the air.

The physical principle of lift is why a sailboat can sail upwind, and it is also why it can outrun the wind when it sails away from it.

Understanding lift is no mean feat. You can't see it. You can't feel it except in the heel of the boat. It is only in the last century that humans have documented and applied it. Today, engineers go to school for years to learn about it. So do pilots, of course. (It is no surprise that both engineers and pilots are well represented among top sailors.)

So the act of sailing becomes less about setting a sail and steering a course, and more about tiny "trimmings" — adjustments to the sail to find the ideal shape to create the right amount of lift for the given condition. A small sailboat might have a dozen or more controls to trim just one of its sails, many with odd names like the cunningham, outhaul or the vang. The more sails, the more controls. America's successful sailing Olympian Buddy Melges was among the most innovative in adding, subtracting, and reengineering the controls for sail-trim, setting the standard in 1974 that won him gold and still exists today for his class, the Soling. Like Buddy, the best sailors usually don't prefer computers to report performance information; they know that ideal trim is a sensation or a feeling more than a set of known targets and predetermined settings. Since every boat and every sail is different, the state of ideal trim is always specific to the boat. Books are written about many boat designs but usually can't cover every detail. Online discussions between sailors go on endlessly about how to "set up" a boat for various conditions. It can take years of practice on just one sailboat to find optimal trim for that boat.

Sail-trim is only what is happening above the waterline.

Underwater, a sailboat's keel, rudder and hull are in a constant battle with the water, which obstructs, is heavier and has more friction and volatility than air. A sailor in the second stage of study is also working to unleash the boat's underbody from the forces of water. He or she will subtly steer the boat around the waves, not through them. They will also reduce the friction met by the hull by lifting sections of the hull out of the water by shifting movable ballast (weight) around the boat. Sailors call it minimizing the "wetted surface."

Finally, sailors are constantly managing the heeling angle of the boat. Too much or too little are slow. For novices, this explains why sailors "hike," or sit on the high side of a heeling boat. They are both controlling wetted surface and heel with their own weight, effectively integrating boat and body or bodies.

A second-stage sailor also becomes a student of peaceful but productive cooperation. To trim more than one sail, or pull a section of hull from the water, the people onboard must form and act like a team, agreeing to do things like trimming and shifting in concert. So the most successful second-stage sailor learns to lead. They cajole, motivate, respect, reward, share, teach and cooperate, sometimes all within just a few minutes.

Better sailors than I could go on and on about the finesse, the organizational skills and the attention to detail that separates world-class sailors from the rest. Like most sailors, however, I can assure that rough sketches and fine art seem more than a lifetime apart. Like most, I feel as if I won't have enough time to learn it all. Like many, I need to stay focused and there will be times when I need some help.

How many people do you know who can bang out a song on a piano? Compare that with how many people you know who can play Chopin well. Basic skills become advanced skills only when two factors exist: 1) the player makes a large commitment of time to practice, and 2) a mentor guides during the tough transitions.

Things worth a lifetime are things that perpetually challenge and amaze throughout a lifetime.

Complexity is not what makes sailing unpopular; it is one of the prime things that makes sailing great.

CHAPTER 10

Kids and Sailing

The truth about exclusivity and the sailing elite.

RESEARCH REVEALS TWO GROUPS of sailors: 1) the vast majority (92%) who believe sailing to be important to a better off-water life, either for themselves or others near them, and 2) a vocal but small minority (8%) who value it as a personal escape from a land life that feels out of their control.

When asked if and how they would help to improve sailing:

- 85% of sailors said they would take a kid sailing;

- 72% said that they would teach an acquaintance or a stranger to sail;

- 55% said they would volunteer to organize and teach a sailing class;

- 42% said that they would volunteer to run races.

The numbers are essentially unchanged between racers and cruisers, old and young, novices and experts, and in good or bad economies. When asked why, these willing helpers say that they want to share the "quality of life" that they feel privileged to enjoy.

Only 8% said that they would not help in any way. Indeed, some in this group are explicit that nobody should help; they would rather protect against too many people crowding their docks, their boats and their waterways.

What would you be willing to do to help to increase participation?	
Option	Percentage
Take a kid sailing	85%
Teach an acquaintance or stranger to sail	72%
Volunteer to organize or teach a sailing class	55%
Volunteer to run races	42%
Not interested	8%

Table 2. 2007 Sailing Participation Poll
Number of Respondents: 585

NICHOLAS D. HAYES

Sailing has always been surrounded by an aura of exclusivity, an air of privilege. But the math doesn't support the myth.

I found overwhelming interest in sailors in sharing sailing with others (and three times as many non-sailors with sailing aspirations as actual sailors). Accordingly, I was surprised — no, *flabbergasted* — to find a sailing industry listening disproportionally and keenly to the tiny minority that would limit it, over the vast majority that want to help more people, specifically kids, to sail with them. It seems as if industry looks at Larry and thinks that it is a good thing that he be freed from the burden of company. In fact, it's quite the opposite: Larry would *prefer* to have company; he just has a hard time finding it.

During research for this book, I talked with dozens of organizers, builders, sail-makers, equipment-sellers, every publisher with an English-language publication or website, sailing instructors and event organizers, and I gave talks in the U.S. and Europe. About half of industry professionals told me that, while they "hope more kids would sail," they didn't see how family sailing would work. Not enough time. Not practical today. Too complicated.

I was told, "We're selling a *adult* lifestyle. Kids don't fit in. That's why they have junior programs."

I was reminded by one industry pro to "follow the money. The boomer's kids are grown." Since boomers have the money but not the kids, sailing can't be about the kids. Let someone else worry about training the next generation.

But this is so clearly a long-range problem for both the pastime and the industry that depends on it. Find a culture where kids and adults are segregated, and you'll find a culture on life support.

To be fair, markets never see far into either the past or the future, and so industry's offers always reflect present customer demands. Here we have a perfect storm: a dwindling pool of avid sailors, and a shortage of devotion from newcomers met with products, services, and programs that don't require any.

The facts? At sailing's peak in the late 1970s and early 1980s (a period of long recession, high inflation, high unemployment and volatile energy costs), more than 5% of Americans sailed, most often (78% of the time) in family groups.[13] Today fewer than 2% of Americans sail, and only

----

13 Family sailing has been a small-group recreational activity and also has succeeded at the highest competitive levels. Sailing was the first sport to bring Olympic gold to a family team: in 1948, father and son Hilary and Paul Smart did it, and father and son Bill and Carl Buchan did it again in 1984, although in different classes.

NICHOLAS D. HAYES

a small fraction of those (less than 10%) do so in family groups.

There is a direct and visible correlation between the health of a pastime and the make-up of its groups. These data plainly show that sailing had a role in American culture for a time when sailing was multi-generational. They also shows that sailing has lost its place ever since it was divided, both by sailors and by the industry bending to the charter, into kids-only programs and a so-called "adult lifestyle."

Sailing isn't alone in American pastimes in the development of junior programming as a theoretical feeder for long-term interest. It does, however, deserve a special award for creating extreme isolation between adults and kids, when it has the least reason to do this. A sailboat might be among the best platforms on which generations can gather and learn from each other, but sailing hasn't taken advantage of this tremendous, built-in opportunity.

In most sailing clubs today, the kids show up in the morning, and leave in the late afternoon, just about the time the adults are arriving.

On most sailing boats underway with more than three people onboard, you'll find nobody under the age of about 45.

In most races, except those created specifically for kids, there are no kids.

The facts are not lost on everyone in the industry, I am relieved to report.

- One of the most popular threads in the wildly active online discussion forum at SailingAnarchy.com is called "kids on boats." There, proud sailors post pictures of toddlers in sunglasses and slickers on all sort of sailboat. In fact, while the site is chock-full of irreverence, one finds ample evidence that its members tend to credit their parents as the source of their own passion for sailing, and hope to return the favor.

- Just this spring, my own club voted to ban smoking on the grounds, including in the bar. The ban is not to punish smokers (of which there are many), but to make the place more welcoming to families.

- A popular new boat designed in France combines a small size and price, safe speed, a private and large bathroom, a pizza oven, a wide-open cockpit that feels a bit like a playroom, and a large retractable canopy. It can be pulled behind a small car, raced, cruised or camped by a family of four; and offers both speedy excitement and the fun feel of a pop-up tent camper.

- A boat dealer frustrated with systemic separation of grandparents, parents and kids by industry structure offers free advanced sailing lessons (many months long) for families as a *condition of sale*. His belief is that everyone needs to know what they're doing, if everyone is to agree to sail together.

Green shoots of change? Will they grow into something meaningful? To tackle that key question, we need to focus away from the past, away from the role of industry, and focus instead on why we should sail together.

CHAPTER 11

Shared Belief

For some sailors it isn't an activity, but a belief system that values "time over things."

....

SOMETIMES WHEN SAILORS ARE seen standing around the beer keg chatting after an afternoon on the water, it is easy to assume that sailing is more an excuse to party than a cultural pathway. In moments like these we forget that these folks are united around a single, bigger idea: that sailing is a better way to live than not sailing.

One sailor I interviewed explains: "We revel in a connection to the cosmos on an ingenious machine that steals sparks from the air and spins them into speed. It's like we're riding on energy that might have originated far out in space. Who knows where it came from? But we all know that we're damn lucky to be on it." Sailing is so crazy and cool that they make time for it. Bar talk is just the archiving of the better moments.

It may seem counter-intuitive to think that geared-up sailors might value time over things. "Time over things" would seem to reflect Buddhist philosophies more than the thinking of the American consumer. But here at the post-sailing beer keg, we find them rallying friends and family, centering on one thing, striving to perfect it by sharing secrets and hoping the day won't end. Almost everything about it is against the grain. At least today's grain.

As a researcher, I have often daydreamed about an economic experiment that would identify the moment in American history when the majority of us switched over from a "time over things" belief system to a "things over time" belief system.

My hypothesis is simple. It suggests that before World War II, when it was unclear whether the industrial revolution would benefit all or few, the general population's largely unmet aspiration was to be in the middle class, with middle class defined as long-lived and free-to-choose. Many fell short, but their kids got the message. So after the war, as the technologies of war found peacetime uses, the next generation built exactly that. The images of the weary faces of their parents etched in memory, these new parents weighed time with friends and family on the same scale as personal wealth and material things, and time often won. So the work week shortened, and incomes rose.

I propose that postwar prosperity wasn't built on the backs of pure human labor and long hours, but developed *because Americans were motivated to be more productive in their work time to earn more free time.* So, with the postwar generation and their kids, we saw things like sailing and fishing and other forms of populist culture springing up to shape our national priorities.

In the last thirty years, the scales have tipped, and the time-versus-things equation now works against us. Sometime between 1975 and 2005, more Americans embraced the idea that a collection of things equals quality of life. Now we trade time to amass our vast collections, and then trade more time to cover the debt service even if the things we have are not useful anymore. At its apex, this sad ideology became the warped, rampant debt-fueled consumption of the first part of the 21st century, when for the first time since 1929, consumer debt equalled gross domestic product.

Now, we find it impossible to use work to earn time. Instead we have to work longer to maintain our stuff. We feel busier, but at the same time shallower and less important, less connected and less productive than ever. With these generations, we see things — like a monthly subscription to reality TV, mall park stacked on mall park, 60-month upside-down SUV leases and celebrity culture myths — exploding and shaping our souls. Time is our afterthought, and the lovely ways we filled it for a few decades have been overrun with trash.

My hypothesis resolves to this: the frightful realities of terrorism, war, climate change and economic hardship may reverse the tide of a "things over time" belief system. Some of the young people that I met while researching this book seem to be much more aware that their time is finite and, as a result, vastly more valuable and precious than I would have considered it at their age. And I won't discount the potential of Americans to learn and adapt, even late in life. I've heard many fifty-somethings say that it is time to seek normalcy in life-priorities, and that they are ready to get to work to do that. We may be learning through a tsunami of bad news and threats that "time over things" is and always was a healthier way of life. If we do, I suggest we will also learn that it is the real meaning of prosperity.

Or not. The cynic in me also sees a sad and scared bunch of Americans, perhaps the majority, waiting it out. Waiting for the other financial shoe to drop. Waiting for the next terrorist attack. Waiting for the economy to improve. Waiting for the kids to grow up and get out of the house. And in waiting, *choosing to let the time pass.*

Sailors often speak of the mystical, the sublime, the magical things that they see and feel while sailing, like the potential of a boat to go faster when the wind it produces adds up to more than the wind around them. Or the feelings of trust and triviality that can only come on a small boat clawing upwind far out of sight of land and under a sky full of stars. Or the sensation that nudging forward or back an inch can set the boat free. Or the rhythmic pitter-patter from the swell lapping at the aft underbelly of an anchored boat at night. Sailors find God in such things. Sailors will often say that they are in heaven, here and in this time.

This leads me to a second researcher's daydream. What if scientists convincingly confirmed that this lifetime *is* our time in heaven? Would more people value "time over things"? What could we expect if they did? Prosperity? Peace? *Could peace be an outcome of the pastime that lasts for life — the Life Pastime?* This depends, I guess, on what you believe.

In the end, one truth sidesteps all research and all science: God or not, DNA, variations, environment and luck create the amount of time we will have here on earth, leaving us with one simple decision. How will we use ours?

Part Two

*About Time and Pastimes,
and a closer look at our commitments
and how they matter.*

CHAPTER 12

Five Factors Influencing Free-Time Choices

The truth about what prevents more people from sailing.

THIS WRITING WAS AN item on my to-do list when I took a day off work, caught a train and two cabs during a snowstorm to travel from Milwaukee to Chicago to attend the annual Sail Expo. The Expo fills the hall at the end of Navy Pier with sailboats and gear, so that weary wintering sailors can start to set their sights on spring.

The day was awful. A big low sat on Chicago and dropped wet, cold and snow in sheets, so the show was poorly attended. Walking the empty indoor mall on the pier in search of a snack, I caught a glimpse through a window of a man at the water's edge, leaning against the icy dock-line of a tour boat, casting bait into Lake Michigan slush. He had ridden his bicycle to the lakefront through deep snow and Chicago's downtown traffic, hoping to snag a big brown trout. His hat was covered with snow. Mittened hands fumbled with the reel and line. I wondered briefly if he was homeless or otherwise on the down and out and in search of food. A new mountain-bike, carefully chained, designer mountaineering jacket and carbon fishing-rod answered that. He was just fishing. In a *frickin' blizzard*. He had chosen to make the trek to the lake and was choosing to stand in the cold, to satisfy a deep desire to catch an old, cold, inedible stocked fish. He was living his passion.

On one hand, a pastime is a way to occupy time. On the other, it is a way to be happy in our time. Many of us have a variety of pastimes, some that we just *do* and some that we are *drawn to do* for deeper reasons. Others may look at us and wonder, as I did spying the frigid angler, why we would ever make such a choice.

Five factors influence our pastime choices: real available time, groups, attractiveness, saturation and programs. Let's tackle them, one at a time.

Real Available Time

If American sailors are an indicator, then many Americans spend an inordinate amount of our free time thinking that we do not have enough free time for our pastimes. If you ask people interested in sailing what prevents them from trying it or from sailing more, only 10% will name an insurmountable financial, emotional or skill barrier. About 55% say, instead, that they do not have enough time.[14]

While it is true that the key to having a pastime is having free time to begin with, it is also true, albeit a surprise to most of us, that Americans have loads of it. With scant differences between income, age, race or region, Americans spend more time doing things that are optional than any culture in history, with the possible exception of our modern counterparts in Western Europe.

If we subtract the activities that are required to sustain healthy life, including our time spent at work and gathering food, nesting and resting, we are left with ample discretionary time. According to the Bureau of Labor Statistics, 45% of waking hours are consumed necessarily, and we can chose how we spend the other 55% of our waking hours each day.[15] After all requirements for living are met, we Americans have 38 hours in a week to use as we wish, including weekends.

---

14 "2006–07 Research of American Sailors," Author's Primary Research. Number of respondents: 1,185.

15 "2006 American Time Use Survey," U.S. Bureau of Labor Statistics.

The real issue is that we are sloppy with our time choices in some large and small ways.

First, to the large: Americans have been choosing to live and work farther apart for the last fifty years, effectively giving their time to the commute required to get back and forth to work or play. Due to the fact that early settlers lived close to water highways, most older U.S. business centers are within sight of a navigable body of water. Unfortunately, today's urban sprawl has moved most homes farther from water, leaving many cities and shorelines empty on nights and weekends. The march outward continues relentlessly, and as it does, free time disappears.

Curiously, the tragedy of 9/11 nudged a few of us out from behind the windshield. Sailboat brokers, as well as camping-tent makers and guitar shops, reported a spike in sales the following spring as a new wave of mid-to-late fifty-somethings reevaluated and tried to reduce their work week of fifty hours (plus drive time of twenty hours).

However, it did not stick. The added cost to keep a boat, the distance to water and the time required to find other people to sail with popped the little bubble. For all of its billing, 9/11 is rightly explained as an event, not as a condition. As it slips into the past, it inevitably exerts less force on our psyche.

For most of us to become aware of a given problem with time management, like the hours we commit to a daily commute, we require some sustained force, like many years of high gas prices or a long recession. One of my favorite statistical tidbits is that the family picnic and pickup sandlot softball game gained massively in popularity during decade of the 1930s, for lack of anything else to do for fun that cost so little. While we cannot underestimate the pain of the Great Depression, we can still find good in the real health of the American family and local communities in the years that followed it. Is it any wonder that what we now call "The Greatest Generation" was taking cues from its mentors during this tough time?

Today, fifty years of sprawl and the vast resources it consumes (and the complex time-habits that it demands) will take a long time to unravel. There are tiny signs that it has begun. Months into the housing bust, researchers compared housing values to commute times in six U.S. cities, and found that houses that were located an hour drive from a city center had suffered a 40% drop in value, while houses within the reach of urban transportation had not depreciated or had even increased a bit in value. If this trend holds, it would indicate a sea change in American access to real available time, after fifty years of chasing the farthest edges of the human community.

Coinciding with this urban sprawl is a dramatic redefinition of family life. At the same time that we've moved outward, women have moved into the workplace in droves. Many economists agree that the first factors leading to prosperity and peaceful governance are mass literacy and an equal right to work across genders. But family dynamics are latent; women still frequently do the most housework and provide the most care to children. The extra burden is especially apparent when children are young and highly dependent. When childcare becomes a part of family life, the commute is often extended by another leg, so parents may spend even more time behind the windshield. The end result is that for at least one member of a two-income family, it feels as if there is no free time at all. And for the rest of the family, overlapping free time is a rarity.

On a much smaller scale, much of the stress that we feel from a perceived shortage of time comes from the fact that we spend a huge slice of our remaining flexible time making largely inconsequential personal choices that may not be satisfying. If we select, for example, to switch on CNN or Fox although we might prefer to be gardening, we are also effectively signing up for a charter. *We are choosing to let the time pass.* We let others fill the time for us. These basic decisions, our disappointing choices and our subsequent quiet remorse, create an ugly cycle of inaction and can dominate our leisure lives. While we typically feel regret having wasted free time, we make these lackluster choices anyway because they seem easier than the alternatives.

Our little personal cycles of waste are not without large, unpleasant consequences. Poor time choices, large or small, can combine to destroy a lifetime, split a family and even fray an entire community. It becomes a closed loop of laziness that feeds on itself. Most often when we choose to do nothing, we're also choosing to do nothing alone. And if so many live in self-prescribed isolation, it becomes easier for any one of us to choose to do nothing, as it has little effect on those around us.

Conversely, one recent study[16] explains that happier people watch less television, and then happier cultures emerge. (Can you believe it?)

Groups

So why not just pick something better to do? Well, we have already suggested that it is harder. What makes it that way?

To start, for most of our 38 free hours we cannot choose anything other than the simplest activities without asking

---

16 "What Happy People Don't Do," John Robinson, Professor of Sociology, University of Maryland.

others to play a part in our plans. Since we frequently move in groups, sometimes as families, sometimes as friends, a choice is often an act of consensus and compromise rather than a personal preference.

A decision that affects more than ourselves can be exponentially harder. In a marriage, if both spouses work, then coordination is made much more difficult by calendars that don't sync well. In a family, different kids and age ranges bring different needs and interests into the mix. We have to multiply the consequences and preferences felt by each of the people in the group to understand the vastness of the options, the complications and the trade-offs. Once we have finally meshed calendars, then we have to motivate the group. "Herding cats" comes to mind.

If you ask sailors who are also nesting parents what prevents them from sailing, intersecting time shortages dominate. Almost 90% of would-be sailing moms and dads don't go sailing because they can't achieve consensus.[17] When they say they lack time, they often mean that others in the family introduce other choices that may seem easier or more important to select at the time.

---

17 "2006–07 Research of American Sailors," Author's Primary Research. Number of respondents: 1,185.

For parents, allocating time to a preferred pastime depends upon whether it is structured and attractive enough to everyone to be done together. And it depends on whether somebody else's pastime choice is calling more loudly.

Attractiveness

Social experts call passion for an activity "avidity." This means that the participant likes to do it enough to choose it over another — or at least to nominate it as an option when moving in a group.

Subjectively we can learn whether one is avid or not about an activity if we ask the simple question, "Which best describes your interest in [name your activity here]?" and provide a range of possible answers that tie time with priority.

A 2005 study of almost 300 amateur racing sailors found that a whopping 52% race as often as opportunities allow.[18]

[See Table 3, next page.]

....

18 "2005 Sail Racing Participation Study," Author's Primary Research. Number of respondents: 282.

What best describes your interest in racing sailboats?	
Option	Percentage
I've tried it once or twice	5%
I go when I am asked or invited	10%
It is one of my hobbies	33%
I race every chance I get	52%

Table 3. 2005 Sail Racing Participation
Number of Respondents: 282

Of course, some might conclude that such personal passion lays a strong foundation for growth in an activity, if it can pass the aforementioned group tests. But if avidity were transferable, then I'd have expected to find a line of people fishing and braving the storm on that winter afternoon on Navy Pier.

As it turns out, it is very difficult to spread one person's passion into a pastime for the masses. In fact, avidity usually develops one on one, or one to a few. (More on this later.) In the end, available time, pressure from family and friends, and the avidity of the participants does not fully explain the health of a given pastime. Something else drives its growth, or decline, and its value to the participants.

For the purposes of distinguishing between our simple and our complex choices, let's call activities that do not require much effort or agreement from others "time fillers" as opposed to pastimes. Time fillers are simple options like watching television alone.

Beyond time fillers, we find a wide range of more complex choices. A "hobby" is a selective activity that we might do either alone or in groups to fill our free time enjoyably. We can organize such chosen activities on three scales:

On the first scale, there are hobby activities that have only a few requirements, like sheer physical strength or speed, versus activities that are highly complex and require mastery of many fields of expertise or capability. It doesn't take more than basic concentration for me to play computer solitaire. But to run a marathon and finish respectably, I must strengthen my knees, lungs, heart and mind. I need to learn about diet, energy consumption, temperature and humidity, and how to tackle exhaustion and manage risk.

On a second scale, we might chart the number of persons required to accomplish the task. In sailing it might be one person in one boat or it could be more. In team soccer, it would be eleven players plus a coach, times two. Of course when more people are involved, more disciplines must be conquered, like coordination, cooperation and clear communication, but when there are too many, social value suffers.

Finally, we can add a third scale to represent the commitment of time required to do whatever-it-is well.

One	Skills Required	Many
One or many	Number of People Required	Some
Low	Time Commitment	High
Low	Social Value	High

Table 4. Factors that Impact Social Value From Pastimes

Taken together, we might notice that fewer skills, fewer (or too many) people, and less time tends to result in less social value. On the other hand, more skills, a small group of people, and more time required tends to result in higher social value.

We will call these deeper, richer, socially meaningful activities *Life Pastimes* because, for the participants, they bring real meaning and self worth. And we can place them, along with time fillers, hobbies, and solitary or group activities, on a scale of "easy to hard" things to choose to do.

	Solitary	Group
	Easy ⟶ Hard	
Time filler — Easy	Watch TV or surf the web	Cruise the mall
Hobby	Collect model trains or stamps	Play bingo or join a bowling league
Life pastime — Hard	Train for a marathon	Sail a boat

Table 5. Time Choice Difficulty Comparison

So a Life Pastime is an activity that we might say defines us; it is something that we are drawn to viscerally for long periods in our life, even when it is hard.

Life Pastimes are the things often reserved for our inner circle of friends and family. They measure up as an attractive undertaking, one that we enjoy doing over and over with enthusiasm. It might feel clumsy to admit, "I am a father, a Unitarian and a bingo player," but it seems natural to say, "I am a grandfather, a teacher and a hunter." We often identify ourselves by our Life Pastimes.

In the new millennium, fewer people are embracing a Life Pastime, in part because so many of our other options seem plainly easier.

Saturation

At a gathering of like-age parents, a dad proudly announced that his eleven-year-old daughter had just added speed-skating to her list of weekly sports, which also included softball, lacrosse, team swimming and water polo. His eight-year-old son has his own six uniformed sports. The mom, of course, has a mini-van with a daily delivery route, and has memorized the menu at every fast-food window between sporting venues.

Today's parenting styles suggest that kids should do all things, whether parents contribute to the experience in ways other than transportation or cheerleading or not. Usually not. As a result, many American kids have a full calendar of extracurricular activities until they have either had enough, are distracted, or have been cut from most or all of them in their high school years.

This dynamic appears in the sailing participation data. For the first time in the history of the activity, almost 3% of kids in their middle and high school ages are taking sailing lessons. About 15% of these kids continue to sail into college. Then, as if to say, "That is enough of that," almost all of them quit and never return.

This is not just normal attrition, it is a mass exodus. It is not caused by burnout. Young sailors that leave say that they feel a strong preference toward things that are either more entertaining (90%) or more meaningful (10%).[19]

Since sailing programs can run out of ways to entertain, then feel like work, it is easy for those kids to look elsewhere for the next dose of exhilaration. Since a sailing program can feel a lot like Little League, it is logical to replace it with something that matters more, like the Peace Corps or Graduate School, when one ages out. Finally, since a sailing program is something that the child does and a parent may only watch, there is very little chance (one in twenty) that a child sailor will call sailing a Life Pastime. Said another way: sailing as time filler or hobby is disposable.

Incidentally, social scientists and teachers have long argued unsuccessfully against cheerleader parenting, citing tangible risks like unchecked, turbocharged peer pressures and a warped sense of priority for the child. Especially if poorly coached, a child in this situation will often sidestepping nuanced learning in favor of trying to seek so-called peak performance.

In fact, countless studies show that peak performance in a skill or sport is of the least important outcomes of childhood, far less important than developing strong problem-

---

19 "2006–07 Research of American Sailors," Author's Primary Research. Number of respondents: 1,185.

solving skills or flexibility in times of stress or crisis. And statistics show that peak performance doesn't matter anyway, since the vast majority of kids never achieve it anyway.

Spectating is not good for the parent either. Whereas Danny the racer can improve his performance by tightening his jibe, his mom's only option is to watch something else. More than one mom told me that she felt like she was missing out on all the fun. "Every time I drop him off at a class, I think, 'He's only going to live in our house for four more years. Why am I constantly driving him places and then leaving him?'"

Programs

Would Millennial kids embrace a Life Pastime if the environment were different? The fact is that these kids are no less willing to make a long-term commitment to something that they believe in than any previous generation. It plays out in their defection from junior sailing. There is evidence, however, that the environment in which a Life Pastime can germinate and grow has been altered, so they are not getting the chance. What is missing?

A quick look at the change in participation between 1997 and 2007 in selected physical and outdoor free-time activities among Americans shows that we spend more time on skateboards and in yoga class than ever. However, we have grown bored by camping and hiking, and we're doing much less fishing, hunting and sailing.

	1997	2007	Growth/ Decline	Percent U.S. Population
	(Participants in millions)			
Skateboarding	7.8	11.6	49%	2.60%
Yoga	6.9	9.1	31%	2.40%
RV Camping	17.3	18.2	5%	5.90%
Tent Camping	42.6	43.5	2%	14.50%
Day hiking	38.8	36.9	-5%	13.20%
Backpacking	6.8	6	-12%	2.30%
Fishing	28	19	-32%	9.50%
Sailing	*4.1*	*2.6*	*-37%*	*1.40%*
Hunting	20.7	12.4	-40%	7%

Table 6. U.S. Pastime Participation Trends
Sources: US Census, American Sports Data, U.S. Sailing, NSGA

At first pass, these data might simply suggest that we are tending to select activities that we can do alone, whereas group activities are holding steady or declining. That may be true, but we might also conclude that complex activities that require someone closely involved to lead and teach are the ones at real risk, activities like hunting, fishing and sailing.

Indeed, the leader-teacher — the mentor — is often the key to the Life Pastime. He or she focuses us and, in doing so, reveals a deeper, more meaningful experience. Since the Life Pastime choice is a more difficult one, it must be linked to family, close friends or culture to pull us to do it. This powerful emotional tug is what makes the activity last beyond childhood and mean more to the participant than a sport or a hobby. The mentor is the person who creates these powerful cultural links.

For example, mentors, usually parents, introduce their kids to hunting. Dads, or sometimes uncles, moms or aunts, start with gun safety, then share their secrets for stalking game or places to hide and point out the subtleties of the natural world. Some thirty years later, *driven by nostalgia and by the memories of their own childhood,* the second generation hunts with the third.

Similarly, a Chicago fisherman in a blizzard would not have chosen to fish on that day had he not been imprinted with a meaningful prior experience with a mentor. Chances are he has caught big fish before and in odd weather. Chances are that he recalls catching big fish as wildly enjoyable, partly because the early events were shared and celebrated with a mentor. Chances are that his mentor was his father, an uncle or a close friend of the family.

Later chapters will explore the idea that mentoring a chosen pastime is a key element of effective parenting, a productive and safe society, and even a vibrant culture. For

NICHOLAS D. HAYES

now, let's just look at some of our pastimes in the context of American popular culture.

If you believe the mass media, an iPod and a skateboard are obviously awesome. A green-tea latte, a tanned guru and a yoga mat are plainly cool. Gutting a bunny for supper is apparently not.

So what is wrong with sailing? The answer is clear. Mentors are disappearing, and with them go its greater meaning. Popular culture isn't able to capture such things. Mentoring is off limits to the mass media.

The shortage of mentors and mentoring opportunities are the critical gaps causing the decline of the Life Pastime in America. The Life Pastime will recover if we reconstruct the continuum of mentoring — let's call it the *Lifeline* — while we also deconstruct our obsession with the charter, the easy time-filler.

If we are to share the richness, health, and good that some of us know come from the special ways we spend our free time, we should start mentoring now.

CHAPTER 13

Mentoring is Contagious Enthusiasm

While a teenager hunts with her dad, she might feel scared and cold and be distracted by thoughts of the new boy in class and an empty belly wanting a slice of pepperoni pizza. Thirty years later, her discomfort and boredom are forgotten and replaced with fond memories of time with dad.

P SYCHOLOGISTS KNOW THAT WE think in idealized metaphors of our best experiences with the people nearest to us. Those thoughts define us.

At any one time in our lives we are loosely and temporarily connected to thousands of people. But modern research shows that one person has the emotional and physical stamina to manage only about 150 direct, personal relationships at any one time.[20]

As communication networks collapse, we appear to be able to take on a few more. Recent studies show that for some people, a social network can grow to 250 persons, but after that we are exhausted.[21] For the sake of argument, I will split the difference and propose that most of us engage about 200 people at any one time.

More important, within those 200 there are but a few with whom we share rich and meaningful experiences and whom we will never, ever forget. A special teacher (mine was Lorraine Greenberg). A camp counselor (mine was Jerry Adams). A favorite uncle or aunt. As we move through life, this core group shifts from parents and siblings to neighborhood friends, to college classmates, to spouses and coworkers, and if we are lucky, to our kids and theirs after.

Contrary to popular perception, it is not the activities that we share with these people that teach us life lessons. It doesn't matter if we are fishing or cooking or gardening together. The activity provides the environment, while the people provide the lessons. It is within and through just a few of our 200 or so relationships that we are defined.

....

20 Carl Bialik, "Sorry, You May Have Gone Over Your Limit Of Network Friends," *The Wall Street Journal Online* (2007-11-16).

21 Dunbar, Robin, *Grooming, Gossip, and the Evolution of Language.* Harvard University Press, 1998.

To illustrate: if you want to help kids in cities develop an appreciation of the natural world, of course you will need some vestiges of the natural world in the city. Thus, the park. If you hope that kids will deepen their appreciation by learning more about one natural subject or another, you will create programs in the park. You might find a volunteer who knows about bats to give a talk each Thursday at dusk.

However, the kid who is inspired to become a wildlife biologist with a focus on nocturnal mammals doesn't do it because of the park or the program, but because of the volunteer's *authentic, contagious enthusiasm* for bats. Such expressions play out, not in DVDs or bat-displays, but in catching and cringing, in gently touching and screeching, and in releasing and smiling together in the dark.

When you happen upon a kid with definite ideas about the future, probably he or she has had such an authentic experience and then made an emotional commitment to the activity because he or she wants more of it. Unfortunately, authentic, contagious enthusiasm is getting harder and harder to come by because we've confused the choice with the charter, and spectating with participating, and team sports with teamwork. Finally and most importantly, there is the problem that mentors, the source of such enthusiasm, are becoming scarce.

Where I live, any kid who can swim can go for a ride on a sailboat on any summer day. About 1,500 kids give it a shot through their school or a social agency each summer. This is possible because about 35 years ago, local sailors negotiated with the city for a land lease near the lake, built some sheds and a boat launch, and collected a ragtag fleet of sailboats to create the Milwaukee Community Sailing Center. If you search YouTube, you can find a video clip filmed by local TV news of a culturally diverse group of jolly 9-year-old boys, led by a 15-year-old sailing counselor, tacking a 30-year-old Ensign. It is as thrilling as sailing footage can be — wind noise, motion, timing — all there.

Moreover it is a real mentoring moment. They are all clearly having fun, and they are all learning. The students are serious and organized, and the instructor, who happens to be African-American, is nurturing, patient and proud. The Center has done an admirable job of making some of these moments possible over the years. Many area sailors say they caught the bug there and have sailed ever since.

However, while it boasts cranes, a ramp for people with special needs, and has been raising money to replace its dusty, cramped classrooms, it hasn't found the right formula for growth. Junior students don't often stick around after high school, and few become instructors. Older members join to sail but not to teach; they don't engage with young newcomers. New instructor recruitment has become a limiting issue. So program retention rates, while impressive compared to national numbers, are still flat.

The Center's leadership knows that what it needs: the unlimited flow of authentic, contagious enthusiasm for sailing. To survive, it must solve this critical problem. It understands that a curriculum that put kids in boats by themselves doesn't yield sailors. Additionally it sees that it can't depend on matching old to young strangers, because neither feel comfortable making the requisite commitment. So it is taking bold steps to pull parents and guardians onto the water with kids.

Conditions have to be right for mentoring. Mentoring en masse is inevitably inauthentic. And it fails when mentoring is confused with a place, a curriculum, philanthropy or a social program by well-meaning organizers. Mentoring is not spontaneous either. Both the mentor and their apprentices need to make commitments, agree to schedules and show up.

What are the conditions needed to ensure that mentoring works well?

First, mentoring is complex, hard work for the person doing the mentoring. Mentoring is not rote instruction or skills training; instead, it is the process of loosely guiding someone else to grow and achieve over time. It requires a commitment from the mentor that is usually reserved for one's own offspring. Mentors often think of it as an investment in the future, and so can be highly selective about whom they will invest in.

Mentors are never driven by economics, but always by the progress that they see in their students. Therefore, when a potential mentor sees only charterers — that is, kids who have just signed up (or been signed up by others) to fill a time slot with something programmed — as opposed to potential apprentices, he or she will look elsewhere to find deeper gratification. Said simply, a classroom with eighteen kids, each with multiple other interests, doesn't look like the right place for someone who hopes to pass on something special. Compared with the expectation of sharing an experience on a boat with room for six and roles for all, it is not even close.

Second, the students of mentors have to be willing to commit, recommit and recommit again, even when it hurts. To have a successful relationship with their mentor, they might have to decide not to do something else that they enjoy in order to keep the mentor's focus. Both the student and the mentor have to agree to work together for some time, and as they do, the relationship becomes more complex and risky. Since progress is the reward, the mentor will often challenge the student beyond his or her comfort level, and the student must respond with renewed vigor. The deeper the commitment, the harder it is to give.

All of this can only happen in small groups of the same people over substantial time. It requires familiarity, respect and trust. Everyone must participate.

Spectating is optional but never, ever recommended. Mentors see spectators as a drag. They distract and get in the way of the hard work of sharing knowledge and experiences.

Unfortunately, mentoring has largely disappeared from the activity of sailing. Twenty-five years ago, father and son sailing teams, boys and girls clubs and summer camps made up the core of sailors. Today, few such programs survive. Most dissolved under the weight of a shrinking market with stiff competition. Boomer kids grew up and had fewer children. The kids they had became soccer, baseball, hockey, or Nintendo players with parents as fans, not teammates. People moved away from cities; distance made it harder to coordinate groups. Individuals chose simpler things.

Since sailing usually requires a group, and since recruiting people to sail is work, sailors have shifted to short cruises and day sailing, forms of sailing that require fewer people on a boat to do it. Would-be mentors have been turned away by the burden of finding would-be sailors, and would-be sailors cannot find a place to learn.

It would seem then that a simple solution to increasing participation would be to help people who want to try sailing to find the people that can help them. This is only partly true because the situation is more complex. Real mentoring is harder now due to sharp contrasts in sailing skill and aspirations between the generations. We have shown that some older folks who sail, like Larry, might be unqualified to teach the young people like Danny who decide to engage in sailing, at least in the techniques that are used to sail a boat at its top speed around a race course.

We have also seen that these talented younger people are sailing for vastly different reasons than their parents or grandparents did, so their attraction to the activity isn't as devoted.

On the other hand, the interest is there. For every two people who are on the water in a sailboat on a weekend afternoon, three others say that they would like to be. From afar, sailing still looks attractive, romantic and exciting. It also seems overwhelmingly complex, so starting appears to be hard. People who want to sail need people who sail to help them begin, and sailors who want to grow need experts to lead them.

However, most of those interested in learning about sailing have not found the sailing mentor within their 200 close relationships. That is because statistically there are fewer potential mentors within our network, as once-deeper secondary networks were long ago replaced with mall clerks and soccer coaches and chain-restaurant waitresses. Then, in the off-chance that a person interested in sailing happens to cross paths with a real sailing mentor, how will the mentor recognize the interest in the would-be learner?

Mentoring does not happen easily on its own, without support from a culture and a community that actively encourages mentors and learners to connect.

CHAPTER 14

Drawing a Lifeline

How Anne became a mentor.

ANNE MET HER HUSBAND in college, where they were junior-year classmates. On their first date, Karl took Anne sailing on his catamaran after dark. They left their shoes on the beach, and strapped a bottle of wine in a backpack to the trampoline webbing. For hours, they were alone in the moonlight on the warm lake, jibing from reach to reach, spying puffs to pull the windward ama from the water. Memory made. Wow.

After graduation Anne and Karl married and moved into careers. Karl raced with friends on weekends. Anne would make a guest appearance here and there, but mostly did her own things. They chartered in the Bahamas and on the Baja coast. And then came kids.

Karl slowed his racing to eight weekends a summer. When the owner of the Antrim 27 on which Karl crewed announced his retirement, Karl jumped at the chance to buy the boat. He sold his newer SUV, bought an old Subaru wagon and used the balance for the down-payment. If he could avoid a car payment for a couple of years, he could own the boat outright.

This chapter is not about Karl and his boat. Read on.

Whereas most people choose to sail to be on the water for a day, going here or there, the second largest draw to sailing is racing. About one million Americans try their luck on a race course. About 800,000 are members of a crew, and the other 200,000 own the boat that they race on.

Racing is one of the many ways that people who go for sailboat rides become sailors and create shared memories.

This chapter is not about racing either. It could be about Anne and how she learned to love sailing. Let's see.

Anne arranged with her parents to take the kids one night a week so that she and Karl could race together in the social series. She had never had a regular role on a racing boat until now. She had sailed enough to know the names of most of the lines, sails and parts. She could manage dock-lines, raise sails, grind a winch, and flake a sail. She knew when to ease a sail, how to steer a basic compass course and how to feather in a puff.

Anne's sailing experiences had been centered on her feelings about the chaotic motion of the boat, her fear of unknown consequences should she make a mistake like releasing the wrong cleated line or not easing a sheet enough in a puff. She pictured wipeouts and torn sails and yelling.

Joining a team of racing sailors immediately redirected Anne's focus away from her personal concerns to the world beyond her small corner of the boat. Before racing, a seat in the cockpit was Anne's sailing universe. It was small, cramped, damp and intimidating. Racing required that Anne by circumstance and company look past the sense of falling that can come when a boat heels over.

Her crew-mates, notably a grandmother and lifelong sailor named Janet, nudged her when she was scared. Janet quietly shared with Anne what she knew about the physics of a keelboat, pointed out that some heel is good and too much is both preventable and not as scary as it might seem.

Through Janet's gentle nudging, Anne began to recognize that when she tensioned or eased a sheet, she could take control of the heeling sensation, but more, she could affect tiny increments of acceleration or deceleration. She watched other teams make mistakes and recover.

Janet met Anne's concerns with clear explanations and hands-on demonstrations. Anne learned to sense when the boat was lumbering, and when it was grooving. She learned that a broach, a sailboat's equivalent to a car skidding out of control for a few seconds, was not as bad as it sounded. Eventually she came to love the action and loudness of a packed starting line, the sensation of unrestrained power and speed when the boat launched off an overcoming wave, and mostly the way that the team worked together to solve problems, and then talked about better ways afterwards, as the sun set and they cruised home.

Within a year, Anne grew from passenger to key member of an active racing team on her own boat. She could identify the favored end of a starting line. She could call a close port crossing. She could sheet a jib from one tack to another without giving up too much boat-speed. She could see the wind on the water, call puffs and lifts and knocks. With her skills came an entirely new level of enjoyment and massive doses of self-confidence.

The next year, Anne entered their boat in the women's Monday night racing series. The following year Anne and her team won the overall trophy. Her crew included Janet and Anne's fearless daughter Abigail (the fourth grader that you've already met), age ten.

Anne's sailing breakthrough reminded her of her experience as a young piano student. From the time she was nine until she was fourteen, Anne met weekly with old Madam

Feckstein and pounded out scales and rehearsed "Minuet," *The Sound of Music* and Beethoven's *Ninth*. Under Feckstein's tutelage, playing in front of people meant playing the whole piece, whatever it was, without making a mistake.

When the Madam retired from teaching, her parents looked for a new teacher and found Miss Morgan, a graduate student of music performance at the nearby college. At first Miss Morgan seemed strange. She didn't assign pages from the *Progressive Learning for Piano, Book VIII*. Instead Miss Morgan brought new and interesting music for Anne to try, pieces by composers she'd never heard of like Perle and Brubeck.

Miss Morgan asked Anne to think about what each composer was trying to say in his music. Once they agreed on an intended theme, Miss Morgan pushed Anne to add her own voice to the work, building on the base ideas. Instead of banging out a song, Anne began to feel as if the composer was living through her when she played.

In a year Anne's playing reached a completely new level, and a new level again the year after that. She started to stretch the music by applying her own dynamic interpretation. Gradually her performances become emotional, mystical experiences for both Anne and for her audiences.

At seventeen, music became forever meaningful for

Anne and she went on to earn her master's in music composition. Anne is a music teacher at the local middle school.

Racing can be to sailing what creative license is to music. It can be the key to unlocking the emotions and emotional benefits that are buried somewhere within. Racing brings nuance, color, progressive challenge, and the frameworks that deliver vast improvements to an already enchanting activity. By its structure, racing can provide an environment in which individuals can explore new territory within the safer confines of a small group of like minds. The result can feel extraordinary, not just to the sailor, but to the entire sailing team.

For Anne, racing sailboats is rich enough that she routinely nominates it as the annual family vacation, and considers it a form of supplemental, vital schooling for her children. Her social network starts on the boat, and builds at every destination she sails to.

Racing catapulted sailing from boat ride to a platform for lifelong education for both Anne and for her kids. For Anne, this would not have happened without Janet's mentoring.

Let's close this chapter by saying that racing isn't the only path to enriching the sailing experience. Other forms can do just as well. I suspect that blue-water sailing, gunkholing and living aboard can serve the same purpose. We'll leave those stories to more qualified storytellers than I.

The key is that even as one can have fun as a passenger, devotion is unique to participants, especially for those lucky to find a mentor like Miss Morgan or Janet. Of course, a mentor's devotion strengthens in the process, too.

So this chapter was not really just about Anne either. It was as much about Janet, Anne's mentor, and about young Sammy and Abigail, Anne's two children and new apprentices.

We are beginning to look more closely at what I've called the Lifeline — the mentoring continuum — seen in practical terms. Real-life examples offer the clearest clues to show how the Life Pastime, through shared memories, is a key transmitter of culture, and therefore, meaning.

CHAPTER 15

Friends on the Water

Ernest Franklin Lipinski passed away quietly after a year-long battle with lung cancer at the age of sixty-four.

E RNIE HAD ENLISTED THE day after Pearl Harbor and was a ship's mechanic in the Pacific Theatre in World War II. After the war, he married his neighborhood sweetheart (and fourth cousin) Bernadette and took work as a machine operator in a Toledo factory, making gears and pinions for truck transmissions.

On weekends he tinkered on wooden boats with his Navy pals, Walter and Francis. First, they each built a rudderless outrigger beach canoe, modeled after those that Francis had seen on Guam's Matapang Beach. One sunny afternoon Walter added a mast and a secondhand sail to his and blasted away from the beach.

Within ten minutes of launch, the outrigger exploded into splinters from the pressure, and the canoe capsized a mile off shore. When Ernie and Francis pulled Walter grinning and shivering from the water thirty minutes later, they knew what to do without saying. The next week they split the $90 cost of the plans and the next winter, each built a Thistle, a 17-foot, three-person, open-cockpit sailboat that Ernie had admired in *Wooden Boat* magazine. They used Walter's basement workshop to plan and fashion small parts, and assembled the boats in a pole barn in his backyard. They called themselves the Warszawaz Sailing Club after the Southeast Cleveland Polish neighborhood of Ernie's childhood.

Walter had two sons. Francis had one son and an assortment of nephews. Ernie had a daughter, and she had friends. They met every weekend, kids in tow, first to build the boats and then to learn how to sail them and eventually to hold races and picnics afterwards. Within five years the fleet grew to fifteen boats, and after ten years to twenty-five boats when the first fiberglass Thistles appeared. The club expanded to ice boating so that they'd have a reason to get together in the winter.

Before cancer took Ernie's breath, Ernie called on his Warszawaz Sailing Club cofounders to "raise a glass and spread my ashes at the Toledo Harbor Light."

＆

Thistles and racing and iceboats were but distant memories when Walter and Francis met at the club bar early on a November Saturday, wearing foulies and carrying Ernie in a coffee can. An ugly northeaster had set in the night before, and spray lashed at the break-wall and the bar window. They would need more hands for the task, so Walter opened a tab and began a round of toasts to their old Commodore. Within three hours they had three willing, albeit teetering pallbearers.

Francis's stout and steady C&C 27 sailboat backed off the mooring and strained to find forward motion against the twenty-knot wind buffeting the basin. The harbor entrance greeted them with 25-knot blasts and breaking gray waves square on the nose. Francis's firm grip on the tiller kept the bow to wind, while the crew unfurled enough jib to steady the boat and provide a bit of drive, even if they would have to tack to get to the buoy a few miles offshore.

The crew huddled in the cockpit and listened while Walter recounted the demise of Ernie's first Thistle. Racing in conditions not unlike these, a few in the fleet had found themselves chasing a left-side shift that brought them precariously close to the shallows at Turtle Island. In a northeaster, waves travel the length of Lake Erie and plow into the shallows near the shoal. The longer a storm lasts, the higher the peaks and the lower the troughs.

Walter recalled catching a glimpse of Ernie's bright yellow boat lifting over the back of a big wave, and then disappearing completely from view on the other side. He looked away to focus on his own driving problems. A minute later he looked back and instead of spotting a yellow boat, he counted six waving arms in the water, disappearing and reappearing among the big waves.

Ernie's boat had dropped into a deep ravine between swells and squarely onto a huge underwater rock, and came back up in splinters. Walter tacked immediately towards the swimmers and hailed the other racers to abandon and assist. Thirty minutes later, Ernie and his crew were safely rescued by their competitors. Pieces of the boat washed up on the shore for a year afterwards. Ernie built a brighter yellow replacement that winter, and the club deemed the area off limits in such weather.

Francis recalled the year that Ernie suggested that they hold a special "lady's skipper night," a race in which a woman must drive, start to finish. It would be a chance for their spouses or sisters to get out on the water, he said. When the day arrived, Ernie passed the tiller to his sixteen-year-old daughter, a veritable rock-star in the fleet, and she promptly snatched the lead at the start and never let go.

Ernie's Thistle won ten straight lady's skipper championships before the club ruled that the event would be changed to "rookie skipper night," so that others might have a chance to win.

Walter told of the time when they had collected and coordinated all their time off and borrowed an old wooden ketch, 39 feet long, with a galley, head and bunks for a dozen. They spent two whole weeks in July 1973 with combined families cruising past Detroit, through Lake St. Clair, up the Saginaw River and then north across Lake Huron to the North Channel and Georgian Bay, the farthest northern shore of Lake Huron in Canada.

They sighted eagles and bear and elk and otters. They smelled cedar and upland fauna. They caught buckets of rainbow trout two days in a row and cooked them in butter with onions. They watched the green and purple aurora borealis reaching into the stars every perfect night.

Stories of Ernie were interrupted by a ringing bell. Francis luffed the boat head to wind and whispered "Ernie, we're here." They started the motor and furled the jib and Francis handed the wheel to the most sober bar recruit. He and Walter clipped themselves into the jack-lines just in case, and climbed out of the cockpit and shuffled slowly to the foredeck.

They didn't say anything. The wind said it for them.

Francis held the bow rail in one hand and Walter's arm in another, while Walter removed the coffee-can lid and presented Ernie to the sky. Then Walter tipped the can over the port rail. Ernie was caught in the big breeze and instead of descending gently into the water, Ernie lifted into the air, hung for a second over his pals, and dropped all over Francis and Walter and the wet deck of the boat.

"Aw shit, Francis," Walter said, "now we're gonna need a bucket." So Ernie was washed off his friend's faces, off the boat and down the scuppers into Lake Erie, one gallon of cold lake water at a time, while his friends grinned and shivered. Then they unfurled the jib and surfed home.

Today, when Anne, Sammy, Abigail and Janet happen to sail near the Toledo Harbor Light, Janet pulls a full can of beer from the cooler and tosses it at the buoy while they all raise a hand in a toast to Ernie.

If the beer can happens to split open on contact, Janet shouts, "Opened it for ya, Dad," and the kids cheer and laugh, and wonder what Ernie was like.

CHAPTER 16

Coming Together
or Falling Apart?

In the last century we conjured up such categories as yachting and yacht racing, sailing vacations and timeshares, windsurfing and regattas, passage-making and day-sailing; all just branches connected to the same tree. Its tap roots are transport, and its trunk is made of people working and learning together on a wind-powered boat.

FIRST THERE WAS SAILING as transportation, reaching back thousands of years before writing, guns and currency. Until the twentieth century, sailing evolved little, but yielded much. Horizons came into reach and, with them, we began to understand our earth and its ecosystem, our species and its relations and our own limitations and new ways to make up for them.

Through sailing, we learned new ways to preserve food. We learned to make maps. We learned to catalog and share our adventures. We learned to harness free energy and to save time, and we learned to conserve energy and make better use of our time. We learned to look to the sky for answers, not just with questions.

Then, sailing as transportation was made obsolete by mechanization and cheap fuel, first coal and then petroleum. At that point, moving about in boats with sails became a way to pass the time for people with some time to pass. For them, sailing has become many things: a weekend away, a way to decompress, a thrill ride, a challenge. And it is sometimes a competition.

When a pastime evolves to sport, it takes as many forms as there are competitive ecosystems to support it. As such, sailboat racing offers almost endless possibilities: social racing, club racing, match racing (equal boats pitted one-to-one, like Thistles), the regatta (sailing's version of a tournament), or offshore races that might take hours, days or weeks. It can be done on a small budget and a small scale, or it can consume a wealthy person's life and net worth.

A few races (less than 2% of all starts) are major media events, hosted by professional managers who provide services like entertainment, provisioning, coaching and photography, who rally spectators and sponsors and publishers, and promise branding on a large scale. These are the exception, not the norm. But these are also the events that most will see in a late-night mention on cable TV or in the very back and bottom of a sports page and that shape the public's view of the sport.

The vast majority of sailboat racing is far more modest. It starts with two or three people saying, "Let's go here to there and see who gets there first." It quickly evolves into something more complex and interesting. Since racing often involves an assortment of buoys to define a course and time-keepers and observers to set starts and finishes, most events are the product of systematic volunteerism. Many yacht clubs can trace their roots to basic race organization, often provided by member-racers who take turns setting buoys and taking time to make racing possible for their competitor-friends. Racing calls on racers to organize.

Most sailboat racers fall into but two categories: 32% who prefer racing identical boats, purely testing the will, skill and luck of the sailors on them, and 68% who sail on a boat designed for dual, triple or more purposes. Handicap racers enter whatever sailboat they have access to and are scored by a system that provides allowances to slower designs and penalties to faster designs.

The handicap system originated to allow people like Ann and Karl to be able to race against non-identical boats and have a chance to compete. Of the 1,200,000 registered sailboats in the Unites States, only about 250,000 are actively raced. Of those, about 80,000 boats meet the criteria set forth by a one-design fleet organization to qualify the boat as equal to its peers.

If you visit any of the online discussion boards regarding sailboat racing, you will inevitably confront a heated debate of the merits of handicapping verses sailing one-design. For the most part, the argument goes like this:

- One-design sailors claim to be purists.

- Handicap-racing sailors argue that their needs are not met by the one-designs that are available to them, or . . .

- . . . That innovation comes from new designs, and handicapping makes the design process cost-effective.

The argument is complicated when:

- One-design sailors start to find loopholes in the rule that defines the design, or worse . . .

- . . . Cheat the designs by adding or subtracting weight or new, unauthorized technologies.

- Handicap-racing sailors lobby for liberal ratings.

- Handicap-boat designers find loopholes that favor one handicap-boat over another.

- Handicapping systems can't keep pace with the rate of design change and become so complex as to become unintelligible.

In the same online forums, you'll find many sailors insisting that their favored sailboat design will be the potential solution to waning participation. As you might guess, one-design sailors want *their* design to be the popular standard, and handicap sailors do not see how a one-design fleet will meet their needs.

In the end, all of this positioning leaves the activities of sailboat racing and sailing in a perpetual state of division. Some have suggested that it's all in good fun. I suggest that it is a drag. Here is data to support my point:

Among 164 U.S. sailing clubs surveyed in 2007, there are 215 different, active one-design fleets, and another three or four fleets each of handicap racers of various pedigree. This means that sailboat racing as a whole has the burden of attempting to appease, or at least juggle, about 500 tiny special-interest groups, some with only a few dozen members but with very definite opinions about what is right and wrong in their sport. It also means that fleets must, by this market design, constantly shrink, rather than grow, to adjust to the latest fad.

So we have hundreds of tiny one-design associations, and sailboat brand owner's groups and handicapping organizations like PHRF, IOR, MORC, IMS, IRC, ORR, etc., etc. — acronyms too many to list.

When the debate overtakes the pastime, the debate *is* the pastime, and the pastime will eventually weaken and may even dissolve. Simple economics support this point. To an eager newcomer interested in the promised purity of one-design, there is the reality that he or she may invest in something that is valuable only to a tiny local group (maybe just two or three friends), that will not transfer well with a move, and will collapse in value when the local fleet starts to fail, which is inevitable. There is also a strong possibility that the aspiring racer will buy a boat and recruit a team, find the time required to rehearse to be competitive, only to find a competitor with an unrecognizable or unfair advantage undermining the good efforts of the others.

Have the branches and leaves forgotten that they are connected to the same trunk and same set of roots?

Sailing is not alone. Many pastimes have been carved into tiny special-interest segments, leaving the segments to argue themselves into oblivion. Let's look at another example.

Wisconsin's lakes have produced bass, crappie, musky and walleye in large numbers for as long as folks can remember. When the season opens, Illinoisans, Iowans and Indianians line up first at the state-line and then at the shorelines for a chance at the big one or to bring home a stringer for a fry. That is unchanged for decades.

The difference today is why they go. Every summer, my grandfather would load his sedan with suitcases, tackle boxes and kids and drive north, where he'd rent a boat at a landing and go fishing for a long weekend. Today, northwoods resorts feature beer sponsors, spas for spouses, game rooms for kids, and parking lots for Tahoes, Hemis and F-250s connected to glossy bass-boats in thirty-two flavors. Some have the American flag in the paint, others sport purple sparkles; some are inboards, others dual-outboards; all designed more for the tailgate party and the race to the hole than the time sitting over it.

When television brought fishing to the living room, it first appeared in a "how-to" format, and then as a reality competition. This made fishing spectators out of cable-watchers and expanded the potential audience for fishing while, at the same time, buried parent-child experiences behind the boat and motor brand. In this case, the charter message is simple and loud: "Get off of the couch and come to where the party is. But first, get the gear because it's gear that matters. If you want to be a man, get ours."

Now, bass fishermen are identifiable and personally committed not to the time it takes to fish but to the make of motor, the tow truck of their choice and, of course, the boat brand that they bought. We have the Skeeter Performance Boat Club and the Ranger Owners' Group, and the Nitro Team and the Triton Club and the Bassdozer Lovers. The bass fisherman's family, it turns out, are not sons and daughters and grandparents, but the other guys who bought a sister-ship from the same dealer.

However, the bass-fishing participation data show that while the would-be bass fishers responded enthusiastically at first to ads on programs, they are now leaving fishing as quickly as they bought into it. The first large-scale layoffs of the current recession happened in the recreational boat building industry. The price of the bass boat has tanked. Fishing, you may recall, is down about 32% since 1997. Only sailing and hunting are down more.

For my grandfather, the decision to fish was a simple reservation of time for friends and sons. He and his friends didn't care how they got there, what gear they would use, or even which species they would catch.

In a charter-driven market, our decisions ignore time and consider instead only brand. As one marketer recently said, "The brand is about the promise of the experience." Notice that it is not the actual experience, but just the promise of the experience. In fact, charterers — people who sell you packages of time — don't care if there is an actual experience, but only that we gear up for it, and select their brand as we do.

So when it finally comes time to fish, we may not go at all. And if we do, our friends and offspring may or may not be a part of it.

In marketing and in charter-speak, sellers deliberately classify customers into distinct and ever-narrowing groups to, as they say, "personalize," to have one person feel special about his or her buying experience. A car with special options. A restaurant with a certain ambiance. A sailboat with just the right interior decor.

To be sure, some charterers are snake-oil salespeople while others honestly believe that their work makes a difference. Even so, the process of personalizing, whether done to scam or to make someone feel special, is counter to a common interest like bass fishing or sailing.

Mathematicians have names to describe trends in group dynamics like these. Fragmentation is when the group is breaking apart, and in doing so, becoming weaker.

Coalescence is when a group is coming together and as a result, becoming stronger. These statistical definitions support business and political models, strategy and responses.

For example, when a market fragments, investments in it might be less risky, since competition is weaker. When groups coalesce they gain buying power, competition increases and prices fall. That is precisely why sailing clubs formed originally; by tapping the buying power of a group, access to lakes and oceans became a reality for the group.

Conversely, when groups fragment, entry barriers like financial or time costs rise. Without a club, an individual has to bear all costs of access, training or coordination. As cost and access barriers climb, popularity must eventually and inevitably drop, although it may not seem so at first.

Since sometime in the late 1980s, many American consumers have assumed that they would have unlimited discretionary income and the ability to buy into whatever activity they wished, without need to share access. A strange period of low-cost borrowing and rapid popularization of inexpensive technology created a false sense of unlimited buying power. During this time, it didn't feel as if there was much need to coalesce, so some clubs witnessed major shortfalls in member recruitment — even as marinas expanded and prices for basic services increased. The average cost to dock a sailboat rose eight times faster than inflation in the last 10 years, even as overall demand measured in usage dropped. Basic supply and demand theory tells us that this had to end.

Now that the economic bubble has popped, the fundamental weakness in this thinking is clear: coalescence is healthy for a community in both good times and bad, but fragmentation is especially visible and threatening in the bad.

In the last thirty years, as fleets and programs have shifted and specialized, sailors have unknowingly carved their common interest into special interests and at the same time have reduced their staying power as a group. The industry, in turn, has reflected those segments in its offers, and has amplified the effect. Fewer people sail, on bigger and bigger boats that consume more and more lake frontage. Sailors with deeper pockets chase design advantages not available to the rest and deter popularization. More people outside of sailing think that sailing is a professional sport of sponsors and celebrities, when, according to the numbers, it isn't and will never be (at least on a large scale).

Most importantly, kids are isolated from parents in programs.

Now, both the pastime and the industry are much weaker than need be. So leaves, then twigs, and then entire branches wither and drop from the tree.

I don't know if a post-petroleum world might reinstate sailing as transportation. It could happen in theory, but probably not in my lifetime. I do know that people with a common interest can agree to be together and reinstate sailing for their own needs: as a good use of their spare time.

The roots and trunk of this tree have not yet given over to the shriveling leaves and bare twigs. But some pruning is due, if only to be reminded of what it is that sailors have in common.

Coalescence means community. It starts with family and friends. It is there, at the base of the grassroots, that groups agree first to spend time together and then spread the idea outward within their social networks. Brothers invite sisters who invite spouses. Uncles invite nephews who invite schoolmates. Mothers invite daughters who invite friends and neighbors. Relationships are created. Groups form. Trust builds. People thrive.

What might motivate them to try?

CHAPTER 17

Remembering Sailing in the Dark

I don't recall why I was alone that night twenty years ago. My wife must've been out of town. I do remember it with crystalline clarity because it was thrilling and terrifying.

WE HAD BORROWED TO buy a 24-foot keelboat that spring. Like a kid with a new bike, I couldn't stay away. I would often try to put myself to sleep thinking about the fun we were having.

On this particular night, with a strong west wind pushing trees around outside my bedroom window, I couldn't sleep. At midnight I grabbed a waterproof jacket and some gloves and drove twelve miles to the marina. I parked in the dimly lit empty lot, fumbled for the gate key, hanked on a jib, rigged and set the mainsail before letting loose the lines and backing out of the slip by backwinding the main.

I luffed up in the channel and raised the jib. From bed to sailing took all of thirty minutes.

The mooring basin floats about 80 sailboats, average about 30 feet long, spaced about 60 feet apart, usually bobbing head-to-wind. In daylight, it can be like sailing through a minefield, and to catch the night breeze, I had to head into it in moonless darkness.

A puff hit just as I got there. I eased the jib-sheet and the boat lunged forward, reaching full speed in a few seconds. It took me more than that to ease the mainsheet and the boat groaned and turned itself up towards a big moored catamaran.

I muscled her back on course, narrowly missing a full-speed collision and shuddered and swore at myself for being so dumb. Why so much sail area? I could have left the jib down until I found the safety of open water, and would have then sailed at a more reasonable pace through the dark busy basin. I had committed and must press on.

By the residual glow of distant streetlights, I could just make out the silhouettes of buoys and hulls emerging ahead. I held the jib-sheet around a winch and then in my teeth, the uncleated mainsheet and tiller in my hands, and I carved up and down and around the shadows.

Sitting out and up on the high side, I couldn't see through the sails, so to identify the next barrier in the maze

I had to routinely turn into my blind spot to expose a looming danger below, hoping it wouldn't appear too late. I worried that a delay between a visual cue like a shadow and a decision to turn left or right would be the tipping point that would cause a crash, and there I would be, alone in the dark in the water. Every twitch seemed urgent. It occurred to me that this was mighty stupid.

And it was so frightfully fun. So when I came to the other side, instead of leaving the basin for the open water as I had planned, I opted to tack around and go back in, this time on starboard. For two hours in blackness, I reached back and forth and up and down. Like a shuttle blindly crisscrossing a loom, I covered every inch of the basin.

When I had safely found and filled every tight little gap with my wake, I found the edge and a clearing, dropped the jib to the deck, then slowly slid between the docks into the slip to drop the main, spent.

I was never more than a half-mile from shore and it only lasted a couple of hours, but it was one of the most terrifying but exhilarating sailing adventures in my experience. Decades later I recall every minute, although, like most people, I can't remember what I worked on last week. Why is this such a powerful memory?

We all commit some slice of our mental resources to the practical guidelines we need to keep our lives straight, like which side of the street to drive on, or which team we favor in a football game, or where the "a" key is on a QWERTY keyboard. Scientists call these our semantic memories.

Mine apparently failed me that night: I should've known better than to sail alone in a dark high-traffic area. We can, as I did then, override what our semantic memories tell us we ought to do to create other types of memories.

The memories that bring us context, that we *choose to make and save* and that define us as individuals, are called episodic or autobiographical memories. These memories archive informative experiences throughout our lives, and as they build, they provide us with our personal record. Over time we come to know ourselves as patrons of our episodic past, a past that we can deliberately choose to create, one small time-use decision at a time.

However, unlike my recollection of solo-sailing at night, we are usually not alone in the memories that we decide to keep, and we usually don't recall the details as finely as I have here. The telling factor in memory worthiness, it seems, is the emotion of the moment, with *worthiness* measured in personal progress which, in turn, can be measured in some larger societal way.

Going to the store by ourselves and swiping a debit card to pay for two gallons of skim milk probably won't register in our long-term memory, unless we either happen to experience love at first sight with the cashier who later becomes our spouse, or because we are terrified of the credit-card terminal.

When we are emotional, our neurons are piqued, and therefore the chances of innate recollection are much greater. We store vivid, full-color, nuanced records of events that are charged with notable change, or love or laughter, or fear or sadness, whether we want to or not. As emotional levels increase, so does the likelihood that an event will be remembered but, more importantly, that it will be remembered vividly and indelibly.

Take this simple test. Quickly think of a great time you had sometime in the last year, filled with laughter and goodness and leaving you quenched emotionally and physically.

Are you recalling time alone or time in a group? If you are like the vast majority, you've let the mental images of your time spent alone wash away in favor of long memoirs filled with social experiences, because these seem to be the ones that matter and therefore deserve your brain-space. We remember our group time in more detail and more often than we remember our alone time. Why? I suspect it is because usually the alone time just isn't as good.

Time alone is usually boring. When it is not, it might be intense, like something scary, like midnight sailing in a crowded mooring basin. There isn't much in between.

My experience sailing alone, with its vivid memory, was an exception, not the norm. The reality is that as humans, it actually feels unnatural to deliberately choose to be alone.

Alone, our laughter does not have a chance to layer onto other laughter, so instead of joyful and loud, it sounds hollow and forced. Alone, the only consequences of our actions are the cold, natural ones. Alone, we are at the mercy of the darkest places in our imagination where feelings of guilt or inadequacy reign. Alone, we often try to avoid stress, thereby avoiding fear. Alone, we do the things that we have to.

Together we do the things that we want to.

Recently, David Brooks, columnist for the *New York Times,* studying cultures, observed that we are a permeable bunch; we naturally mimic the people around us. He writes that "relationships are the key to happiness," and notes that people who live densely tend to flourish, while "people who live with few social bonds are much more prone to depression and suicide." Why? They don't have a warehouse of fond memories to occupy them in the present and to motivate them to create more.

Then why does it seem that some people go sailing to be alone?

If you ask sailors why they sail, they'll give two answers that are in a virtual dead heat for most important:

1. "[It's a] break from the routine," or

2. "[It's a] chance to see friends.

When I read these answers, I translate them to mean:

1. It's a better way to use my time, and

2. It's even better with people I like.

The vast majority of us seek companionship in our adventures. I sailed in the basin in the dark because I wanted to see if I could do it, but I did it alone mostly because there didn't happen to be anyone around that wanted to share it with me at the moment.

You'll frequently hear a sailor say that time on the water is time away from the distractions of the day. No matter how hard work or school is, no matter what the pressures of the moment, when we are sailing our minds have been transported to a better place. Usually we want to be transported there along with friends. This is because we know that the chances that we will create a fond memory together are much better than otherwise.

To be sure, there are a few hermits among us, notably Henry David Thoreau or, in sailing circles, yogi adventurer Bernard Moitessier. Without exception, these men chose solitude not as a permanent state of being, but as a way of exploring and learning with the intent to share afterward with others what they discovered.

One of my closest friends sailed around the earth by himself. Regular guy Tim Kent, a sales manager and life-long Great Lakes sailor with barely a few weeks of prior solo-sailing experience, raised the money to buy a 50-foot carbon-fiber, single-purpose sailing rocket-ship and hurtled himself into the southern oceans. Alone, he battled serious equipment breakdowns, breakneck speeds, huge waves, violent storms and a year of sleeplessness. Tim's story deserves a book of its own. I will not try to do it justice here. This short postlude will make my point:

After Tim's astounding second-place finish in the 2002/2003 Around Alone race against a small group of talented and bold adventurers, Tim returned to land life exhilarated and ready to build on the experience. He would inspire us with his stories, then create a sequel or two by making a career of such adventures. During the race he kept a careful diary, a long log of emails, and notes, photos, video clips and recordings, stored in duplicate on a couple of laptops that he kept in separate dry-bags, just in case. He had plans to assemble his best stories into a presentation and a book, and to go on tour to raise funds for a larger boat.

However, a few months after the finish of the race, everything was lost when his boat, called *Everest Horizontal,* lost its keel, turned upside down and was scuttled in the middle of the Atlantic Ocean while returning from Bermuda. He and his crew were saved, but his records were lost. Tim felt that, while his life had been spared, his dreams were gone with his hard-drives. He was deeply depressed and lonely for a couple of years following the accident. His friends, including me, worried about him.

A few years before the race, Tim and his wife had amiably divorced. They'd agreed to shower their kids with love as consistently and deeply from separate houses as they would have under one roof. Now, a decade after the divorce and years after the race, Tim sometimes says that he feels lonelier onshore among crowds than he was offshore on a boat by himself.

Physical proximity to people is not the be-all state that creates emotional substance and enables clear memory making. It is possible to be lonely and emotionally flat in groups, just as we can feel one with humanity and alive thousands of miles from another warm soul. We can also feel close to others even when we are not together, and the result is essentially the same. These shared feelings create the connected, collective experience that provides meaning in our lives.

So some sail alone, not to escape company but because our soul-mates tag along vicariously, either as crew-mate spirits from the past, like navy dads, or as listeners to our stories to be told electronically or later in person. In the present, we are emboldened and motivated as if we were muscling the same set of sails and winches.

Nostalgia is how we honor people from the past in our present. Larry daydreams while he sails alone but is kept company by his heros. T.J. teams with Vince and listens for Calayag's whispers when he sails. Had that Chicago angler caught a prizewinner in January, I suspect that he would have shared his joy, at least in his daydreams, with his mentor.

Today, Tim's episodic memories are intact, gradually reversing what might seem like a tragedy of lost records. He regales us with tales of his wild ride around the earth. His stories are rich with immense natural forces, small human desires and lessons for living. I'm hopeful that one day he will write his book so that more people can experience it. Whether his stories reach two hundred people or two hundred million people, they are a valued addition to the human record.

Memories are the human record. And community is fueled by a yearning to connect, to share an experience, even if it temporarily happens alone. In that context, it's easy to see why we should choose our time wisely in our lifelong quest to gather rich stories worth sharing.

Fond memories are the natural and logical outcomes of the Life Pastime. They are the reward that we find for making the big choices and for rallying others to make them with us. When we all have them, they evolve into stories. When we tell them, they shape our culture. When we write them, they become our history. When we reflect on them in groups, they define our values.

Our free-time choices are the cornerstone of both our individual legacies and our cultural capital.

CHAPTER 18

The Value of Time

Almost anyone will say that time spent with a kid is good for the kid. To what end?

A FEW YEARS BACK, LAS Vegas promoters announced elaborate plans to create a "family friendly" area of the city. Charter marketers had identified a market segment of "family friendly" buyers who wanted kids to be nearby but occupied. There, kids watch semi-safe cable TV programming and snack on sponsored packaged foods. The parents go off to gamble. Call it pastime day-care.

At its most extreme, we see padded rooms re-branded as social programs, marketed with scientific-sounding labels like "early childhood social development" to make the parents feel better about dropping the kids off. General day-care psychology aside, the simple and clear lesson learned by the child is that the parent would rather be elsewhere, doing otherwise.

The idea of "family friendly" doesn't always mean separated. Parents can choose to go to a G-rated movie or a pasta-only restaurant chain with their kids. Better to call such things "family safe," where adult themes are veiled into innuendo, flavors are bland and no finger touches a restroom fixture. In "family safe," it is not the time that matters, it is only about basic assurances of sanitation and convenience. When we see a family caught in the "family safe" rut, and there are many, we see mostly boredom and a propensity to choose the easy. Family-friendliness is a memory-killer because it strips away contagious, authentic enthusiasm and replaces it with a flimsy veneer of amusement.

Sailboats are flatly not family friendly in the popular sense. On sailboats, people argue, swear and shout. On sailboats, people fear, cry and celebrate. On sailboats, people fart, burp and vomit. All out in the open. But on sailboats, people, even children, learn to trust and understand each other, even when mistakes are made or common-sense lines are crossed.

Sailboats are family friendly in the practical sense. When things happen that seem out of sorts, sailors explain them and fix them because the consequences of ignorance are too great. So sailors learn to live patiently, creatively, cooperatively and flexibly in their world. Then, later in life, they recall the experiences as rich and formative.

The "family friendly" or "family safe" phenomenon is countered with the idea of "family values," another marketing ploy that destroys memory-making. The phrase family values may have been coined with good intentions. However, not long after it became the mantra of an ideology, it began to suggest a set of restrictions as opposed to a set of tools for living. Family values, as we understand them now, usually include a list of things not to do in life.

"Don't swear. Don't disobey. Don't get fat. Don't think about sex. Don't have sex. Don't miss church. Don't take risks. Don't explore. Don't do anything that I haven't authorized you to do. And then, once you've tiptoed through a minefield of don'ts on your way to adulthood, make sure that your kids hear the same from you as you are hearing from me."

This isn't a culture of learning, it is a multi-generational lockbox.

In societies and in families, behavior throttles like censorship and segregation are mandates disguised as values. We know this because history memorializes one's good will, but regrets most edicts. Kids, especially teens, are rightly designed to reject rules that they perceive to be shallow or baseless, and question the rest. This explains why teens and parents often can't agree on simple things like curfews, clothes or chores.

When we hear the phrase "family values," we interpret it to mean "family rules." When we see a family applying these rules without reason or scrutiny, we are seeing a family that is either afraid of the future, or can't be honest with itself in the present. They may use a bit of time to debate what not to do. But they often can't make the hard choice to be together for the sake of being together.

As a result they lose the chance to confront challenges together because they lose the chance to cooperate to solve problems. Instead, they avoid problems by trying to control the environment. Here, the simple and clear lesson learned by the child is that neither the parent nor the child is worthy of trust.

In a chartered life, we walk from one roller-coaster ride to another in between the yellow "don't cross this line" ribbons. In a chartered life, the rules and paths are laid out for us. Parenting is more about keeping kids inside the lines and moving them forward, than it is about living though original experiences and the making of memories. We select family friendliness not because it benefits the family, but because it is easy and cheap. A junior meal deal contains the same food, includes a toy, and is discounted twenty percent. We talk of family values because we don't have the tools to frame and pass on rich culture. If we are not sure how to approach the subject of chastity, for example, perhaps Hannah Montana can do it for us.

At the same time, kids, especially teens, are sinks for natural and logical consequences, those just outcomes that help them to make sense of the world that they are seeing and touching for the first time.

When we sail a boat or sit over a fishing hole or in a duck blind or play a duet with kids, we are blessed with a built-in set of natural laws, instead of don'ts, that reveal a set of timeless, ageless truths about the human condition, and that we will recall throughout our lives.

- "We will catch a fish if we are patient."

- "If we practice, then we can play a song together."

- "We need the wind, the water and this little boat to get to the other side of the bay. We need each other to do it safely."

Time is the only family measure of value. In fact, it is the only human measure of value, because time is our only birthright. Making the most of it ought to be our only goal. If we do, the Lifeline will take care of itself, and the Grand Benefits will flow uninterrupted.

Part Three

*Mentoring, Life Pastimes,
and other ways to put our free time
back to good use.*

CHAPTER 19

Steps to Make a Life Pastime

Places where sailing, playing an instrument or dancing are not just commonplace but vital, evolving and multi-generational also happen to be places where culture is vital, evolving and multi-generational. If people sail today, we can expect a brighter future tomorrow.

E ARLIER I POSED THE basic question of whether the Life Pastime is worth saving or not. I have argued the case, through stories and facts, that the way we use our free time has enormous positive consequences for us, the people around us, and potentially for the generations that follow. I have suggested that people who embrace a Life Pastime — who choose to fill their time with complex, learned group activities — live longer, happier, healthier and more satisfying lives than those who cannot, do not or will not.

I would suggest then, that it is incumbent upon us to ensure that such opportunities are not lost to an isolated and shallow future. Yes, we must save the Life Pastime to find substance in our lives by reweaving the Lifeline. But how?

Rule #1: Never downplay how big it is.

There is no shortage of audacity among charter-makers in working to remove, lower, or at least hide the barriers to entry to whatever charter they are selling. Have you ever seen a Walmart without ample parking? Flights to Las Vegas are always suspiciously low in cost. "Don't worry, if you want to see the top of Everest, we can make all the arrangements and carry all the gear." Spas, cruise-lines, vacation resorts and theme parks call it "all-inclusive," which means that you do not have to do anything except swipe a credit card to play. Easy is about easing entry and seeking subscriptions. It's never about the people, just the volume. As we have seen, it is not sustainable because, as in the case of sailing, easy isn't true.

If we will rely on the charter to define our culture, we can expect that it will be easier and easier to subscribe to a menu of entertainment options, and we may have gobs of fun as we select and consume. We can also expect that when the freshness fades, we will be left with a large tab and shallow remorse like that of a hangover from binge drinking alone.

Moreover, we should plan for regret or even real hardship if we attempt but fail to break from the charter cycle, or if the charter cycle is broken for us by something like economic hardship, health problems or age. Here we learn too late that days, months, even years were lost. "Oh, shit, I wish that we had done [name your pastime here]. . . ." We can watch our culture erode until it is both unrecognizable and meaningless.

At the same time there also is no shortage of audacity in the choices made by the people you've met in this book. Their first choice was to stand fast against powerful social norms and sidestep the charter, choosing to shape their lives around a better use of time.

- Ron and Jeanne chose to live near the water.

- Danny chose to spend every childhood summer day in a small boat and his parents agreed.

- Vince and Calayag focused all their free time on being with T.J. on the water.

- T.J. focused not just his free time but also a lifetime of work on being on the water.

- Larry learned how to sail alone.

- Francis, Walter and Ernie built boats, clubs and programs from scratch and left clubs, programs and memories as their legacies.

- Karl and Anne saved money and time and rejected the status quo so that they could consolidate their free time and spend it on the water.

- Anne and her children go to a place that most people think is scary and cold, learning together that it does not have to be.

Millions of others make similar bold choices to shape their identities and to assemble a life rich with memories.

People who want to sail or fish or sing together may move to certain locales; they may select certain vocations or reject certain peer pressures. People who want to sail or fish or sing together may risk their retirement, or change course away from other callings, or leave non-sailing, non-fishing, non-singing friends behind.

People who want to sail or fish or sing together will set specific priorities. They will carefully organize and ration all of their time commitments to consolidate enough hours to do what they want to do. They will take time to connect with other people to sail, fish or sing together, planning weeks, months, even years in advance.

Sailors by their nature are a tiny counterculture. They, like other countercultures, protect an ideological premise, such as the idea that a small boat sailed by a small group has social value. Countercultures can either be the inspiration for popular culture or, as we have witnessed, the nostalgic curators of one that is approaching extinction.

If sailors hope that sailing will survive and grow, or if anglers hope that fishing will survive and grow, or if folk musicians hope that playing folk music will survive and grow, then regardless of the format, they will recognize by their own experiences that these are not things to sell or persuade people to do.

Life Pastimes are large, long and persistent choices — often on the scale and terms of a person's faith, health habits or marriage — made by people seeking something larger and longer in their lives and willing to make concessions on the way. As Jeanne explained: "We need to be near the water; it is in our blood."

If sailors hope that sailing will survive and grow, they won't try to convince others that it is easy. They will rightly call sailing what it is: difficult, time-consuming, evolving, sometimes risky and always worth it.

In order for Ron and Jeanne and the kids to find their Life Pastime, they will take stock of the few years left together, find something difficult they can agree to learn together, break old habits and set new, grand expectations.

Rule #2: Share the Grand Benefits.

More than anything, sailors, like others that pursue free-time pursuits with passion, will tell you that they sail to find Friendship, Experience and Freedom. Let us call these things the Grand Benefits of the Life Pastime.

And Grand means big. Really big. We must not downplay how big these ideas are in the context of a lifetime or more. Friendships may come quickly but they deepen over years. Experience may take decades. Freedom may not come in a generation or more, so the generations will have to cooperate to get it. These are nuanced, complex ideas that are hard to conceive, harder to find and can take a lifetime or even lifetimes to confirm.

Grand Benefits span not only generations, but generational attitudes, age differences, educational gaps and economic cycles, and they reach out past the immediate family to the extended family and beyond. But can we realistically expect to share the Grand Benefits beyond ourselves, our immediate family and our inner circle of friends?

Rule #3. Reach to the Outer Circle.

Consider that, with rare exception, when we think of a culture, we almost never think about its jobs and how its people worked, but instead, about its innovations, its contributions to the human condition, and to long-term progress and its spread. Think Ancient Greek; think philosophy. Think Florence at the time of the Renaissance; think unleashed creativity. Think American; think men on the moon.

All have their roots in more refined human constructions than just our employment or gross domestic product. There is no philosophy without scholarship. There is no Mona Lisa without patronage. There is no space exploration without intrepid scientific pursuit.

Further, all are conceived in personal relationships and in the lineage of common interest between just a few people who cooperate to define the counterculture that eventually evolves, grows up, and shapes the culture of nations. There is no Aristotle without Plato. There is no da Vinci without Medici. There is no Armstrong without Kennedy.

What we do in our lives leaves large footprints in our social networks. Our memories become stories, and stories become social history, and history shapes culture. Culture, researcher Hans Rosling points out, is "what brings joy to life; it is the value of living."

I want to close this chapter by directly linking sailing to culture in two steps:

First, when sailing is rightly seen as a real intellectual and physical challenge, worthy of someone's hard effort, their large commitment of time, their athleticism and intellectualism and their teamwork, then it finds its way into our social discussion.

Then, when those who do well at it can be seen to do well elsewhere, sailing begins to have an impact outside of itself. Social value from sailing is sparked in personal relationships. It spreads throughout our social networks in the forms of good decisions, valuable innovations, critical thinking, resource sharing, risk management and fair play.

And, therefore, in all its glory, with all its Grand Benefits, sailing deserves to be shared widely. It will take a lot of mentors to get this done.

CHAPTER 20

Homegrown Mentors

Devotion starts early, and it takes time and the devotion of others to build.

C AMP MINIKANI, ON THE shores of Lake Amy Belle in southeast Wisconsin, has sailboats and canoes, and cabins and tents, and woods and a lake, and horses and crafts and a fire-pit.

Mostly it has kids who want to become camp counselors. They'll do about anything for the chance. They will set aside the iPod and the text message. They will opt out of soccer, ballet, baseball or gymnastics to jump into gooey, cold mud to their shoulders or handle slimy tadpoles and scary snakes. They will spend their own money for the opportunity to wash thousands of dirty dishes or plunge poopy toilets for many weeks. They will leave home and school friends for entire summers during high school, all for the chance to spend their college summers with packs of younger kids on the lake and in the woods.

This has been going on for decades. But it is not your normal summer camp. It is one of those few, special places with an unbroken Lifeline; a 50-year-old mentoring continuum, producing generation after generation of leaders. Campers become counselors, then act as mentors for the next group of campers who become counselors.

Furthermore, with high frequency, Minikani alumni go on to become leaders in their communities. This is exactly the model that one would seek if attempting to build, from scratch, a strong institution of learning and culture like a church, a school, or even a family. How did it start? What keeps it going?

Sometime back in the 1960s, camp managers detected a real gap in the leadership and teaching skills between counselors who had attended the camp as campers and those from the outside who had been vetted through a normal process of reviewing resumes and holding interviews.

So they created a more intentional process to home-grow their staff. It took almost a decade to take full shape.

It germinates when a camper is seven or eight years old, the first years that a child might attend an overnight camp. And it lasts until the child prepares for his or her first year in college, when a few are chosen by older peers for a handful of coveted counselor positions. As trainees and then as counselors, these young adults develop a camaraderie, with a shared goal to make more counselors, and develop friendships often unbroken for the rest of their lives.

The long-term effect has been fantastic. For those who are hired as counselors, the experience is as formative to adult life as any school, church or family activity might be. For those who are not hired, their camp memories remain warm and vivid and influence the other things they do. Authentic contagious enthusiasm, the marker of a mentor, and the social lubricant of the Life Pastime follows Minikani alumni wherever they go and whatever they do in life.

Faced with time-choice complexity, the onslaught of the charter, and the new family dynamics that we have seen throughout American society, Minikani's story is not without its challenges and complications.

Camping organizers and associations have tried many times to recreate Minikani from a template and apply it elsewhere, with little success. In these attempts, the new management of each new Minikani has found it harder than expected to replicate the meaningful connections made between kids and trainees and counselors. And Minikani itself has tried to extend its leadership program to more teens, but has run into some natural group-size and quality thresholds.

This is the classic limiting problem of a centrally managed organization. While it can retain the power of the purse, it is unable to repeatedly create the power of the personal connection, because it is difficult for distant managers to understand how it starts and builds and what sustains it.

Any group wanting to home-grow its mentors needs to begin with an inspired first generation, one with the rare skill to operate at a high energy and emotional level without the benefit of personal attachments to the cause. Imagine trying to assemble the best natural instructors and leaders in a given life-skill in one place, and get them all to embrace the culture of the place as if it was their own. This is a bit like asking a church's members to accept a new theological doctrine. Such dramatic shifts demand the clearest, simplest vision with the boldest, bravest members, and inspirational leadership. For those who will enlist, these can only be big choices. Huge choices. The charter has no place in the conversation.

Then, understand that it is impossible do it en masse. Mentoring can't be scaled up. That is why charterers sidestep it, why they must promise something easier. They are unable to pull it off. Meaningful personal connections are simply not possible in groups that are either too large, too short-lived or too conjured. Too many in the mix always dilutes.

This explains why small class sizes are favored by teachers and by students, and why schools have homerooms. Camp cabins are ideally designed to limit populations so that individuals can thrive. When larger organizations try, they simply cannot produce and reproduce mentoring to the Minikani standard. They can only allow mentoring to happen spontaneously and stay out of the way when it does.

Summer camps or coveted colleges or cultural centers such as museums or junior sailing programs or sailing clubs can just as easily fall into the chartering trap as theme parks or hotel chains — and for the same reasons that individuals fall into the trap. Camps often straddle a gray area between entertainment and experience. They can over-program and come off like a spa. Soccer or hockey camps can overplay and feel like dumbed-down pro football training camps for teens. Soft-drink and shoe sponsors steal authenticity and replace real people with cardboard cut-outs. Parents line up at the gate on the last day of camp to attend the finale game, carrying branded banners and acting more like NFL or NASCAR fans.

This is overt chartering, by design. It is easier to understand marketing and entertainment than it is to understand basic human emotions and manage the risks of mentoring. Chartering and authenticity are like oil and water. Stir all you want, but in the end they can't mingle.

So, a camp like Minikani (or, say, a sailing club or school) can resolve to be about personal growth and learning. It does this by nurturing a mentoring continuum, based on the continuity, sustainability and strength found in a homegrown teaching corps.

Such places and programs reject commercial sponsors and the flawed idea that "bought time" is as good as "made time."

Mentoring is teaching infused with leadership. Mentoring may center on a principal skill or a capability like sailing, but its mastery isn't exclusive to the skill or the technique, but to the broader understanding of what makes the skill or technique valuable and relevant.

Minikani camp counselors don't just teach boating or sailing skills, they teach leadership. They invest the time to accomplish that goal, summer after summer.

Mentoring is also the art of issuing a challenge that is just barely out of reach. Mentors help apprentices understand and set goals. As goals are achieved, apprentices begin to trust the process and the mentor, while improving whatever skill is being taught.

Minikani's counselor track is, at its core, a series of annual checkpoints where candidates demonstrate progress measured in real leadership skills. It is a peer-determined meritocracy, combined with an unbreakable commitment to the complete development of each individual.

Sailing clubs and schools that will survive and grow are those that embrace the Minikani model. They will look past any one season and any one type of boat. They will shed the kids-only model and the limits of a curriculum centered on rote skills or meaningless competition. They won't measure wins; they'll measure themselves on the development of home-grown leaders, generation after generation, and on the social value that those leaders will create in their lives.

The distinctive characteristics of an outstanding teaching institution are:

1. Its ability to home-grow its mentors.

2. Its leaders' ability to defend and protect the continuum.

And here's a key concept: parents can do this, too.

Arguably, it is what parents are obliged to do. And it is the central call to action in this book. Taking a lead from Minikani, parents too can become mentors, as long as they are willing to make bold choices and invest real time.

True, parenting and mentoring are distinctly different roles. A parent does not necessarily make a natural mentor, and vice versa.

We parents intuitively know this, and know that sometimes we need others, like camp counselors or teachers, to help us help our kids have experiences that they will value.

The question isn't how much should we outsource, but how can we be as effective as the best of those we depend on to temporarily assist in our children's development.

How can we get as good as Minikani camp counselors? How can we create our own Lifeline?

NICHOLAS D. HAYES

CHAPTER 21

Becoming Mentor-Parents

Summer camp lasts two weeks. School lasts nine months, and then only five days a week. Parents must first make the time with their kids and then offer opportunity for personal growth and learning during it.

G OOD MENTORING DEMANDS THE confidence of experience. You have to have been there. And you have to want to return to help someone else go there, whether the destination is a place or a feeling or a skill. This doesn't suggest that a mentor must have the same innate talent or be as polished as an apprentice. The mentor only needs to understand the basic environment and the signals within it.

How often have you seen a mom or dad looking more afraid than confident in front of their hollering toddler? How often have you heard a parent of a teen say something like, "He just started to freak, and I didn't know what to do."

When parents don't do things themselves, they don't develop confidence. When they lack confidence, they are left to be afraid of their children, starting when the children are young. If things go poorly, the family might suffer social ills of all sorts. If they are lucky to get through it intact, then the parents are often relegated to the bleacher seats and the kids are without nostalgia and cultural connections.

When American parents assume the roles of taxi-driver and cheerleader, they also effectively take themselves out of the mentoring game and hope for the best. *They are choosing to let the time pass.*

The counter to this arrangement is the mentor-parent.

Mentor-parents start by taking on a greater role than spectator. They have the moxie to reject the all-sports-for-all-kids paradigm, in the same way that Minikani rejected flawed recruitment models. And for some of the time, mentor-parents stop acting only like parents.

For example, the natural parenting response to risk is to avoid it altogether. Parents don't often nudge their children toward what they perceive to be risky behavior, especially at an early age. For obvious reasons, parents are better at shielding. Shielding spares everyone the worry of the terrible emotions that would come from avoidable loss. At the same time, shielding can slow childhood development and leave parents with the burden of regret.

There is much evidence that if a parent isn't familiar with the true risks of something, then they will assume the risks to be much higher than they actually are. So if a parent never sailed, and thinks the lake is dangerous, there isn't much chance their kids will sail either.

Hyper protectiveness is a relatively new development, but it has taken on new life very recently. Large farming families of the mid-20th century in Middle America and Europe, for example, spread risk as necessary to manage the farming operation. Parents acted not just as protectors but as career counselors. Parents could more naturally take such roles because they had been apprentices before and because they knew the objectives and methods of farming.

Now, family farms and family businesses are rare. Today it can be hard for a parent to know what a child might do in the future. Often, parents hope that it will be something different or more than what they did or do, but they're not sure how to provide the guidance.

So we tend to do things *for* our kids and we almost

never do things *with* them. The things that we do choose are those that we think will be safest.

But in a family environment with mentor-parents, as in Minikani's camp-cabin environment, the mentor's approach is to share and to sequence the apprentice's learning experiences — to manage future risk and to hold the interest of both the mentor and the apprentice.

I can hear Anne, working the jib sheet, whispering in young Abigail's ear. "First try a little less mainsheet. Now, hold the tiller more lightly and try again. Good. Do you feel the weather helm? You might try a tiny bit of backstay. See those clouds over there? They might have a bit of wind in them. Do you want to go see?"

I can hear Abigail say, "I don't think I'm ready, Mom," and Anne responding, "No problem, you're doing well."

Wise counsel, next challenges issued, patience, positive feedback. All there. Available only because Anne can be confident in her role as mentor-parent because she herself is a sailor.

Now flip it, and imagine an improbable and awkward scene where Danny says, "Mom, that's way too much mainsheet. What are you doing? What don't you get about weather helm?"

I can hear Danny's mom saying, "Never again," under her breath.

To determine a given family's strength and sustainability on the same dimensions as we measure Camp Minikani's, we would choose similar measures:

- Do social and cultural themes span the generations?

- Are the kids inspired and motivated by these themes to explore and learn?

- Does the family make hard choices in order for the individuals to grow but remain emotionally linked through shared experiences?

- Do the parents grow too?

- Is the Lifeline unbroken?

When you see a family that fits these descriptions — and they are rare — you are also seeing one that has broken with most current American social norms:

- Instead of trying all things, these families choose a few activities and weave them into their lives.

- Instead of buying charters, these families make difficult time-choices and honor shared time most of all.

- Parents invest in their own skills to be able to transfer skills, often concurrently.

- Parents do things *with* the child, not just *for* the child.

Key is the parent's ability to find the right timing and sufficient confidence in the face of strong social pressure to do otherwise. They often understand, at least intuitively, why they must. Parents who mentor determine early that their window of opportunity is small and that much light must pass through it in a short time.

They understand that they have but fifteen years or so when all family members will live in the same place. This is the period in which children are exploring their own physical, emotional and intellectual limitations and virgin creativity and freedom while in the view of caring eyes. These are brief but critical years when lessons of work, play and the consequences of time choices will be etched forever.

So mentor-parents acknowledge the brevity of these productive years. And they seize them and do as much with their kids as they reasonably can, even if they have to quickly develop their own expertise in a skill so that they can share the activity.

It's not a desperate rush to pack things in. It's a long-range vision with a goal to build a strong family by being a family while it is viable to do so.

The tool for mentor-parenting exists: the time choice. It opens the door for the parent to develop confidence, and it signals unconditional love and respect to the child. Used liberally and starting early, a family might just buy a few bonus years later.

A father of a newborn might help the child find fun places to gaze. A mother of a toddler might explore new flavors or words through shared foods and books. A father and his fourth grader might sit in the lounge chairs in the chapter-books section at the library every winter Saturday, swapping titles. A mother who hopes her eleven-year-old daughter will develop respect for her body will herself model appropriate clothing choices, choose healthy foods and activities. A parent with some musical skill might accompany a child in a recital.

A father and mother and their teens might become a sailing team.

CHAPTER 22

Sharing Grand Benefits

Old ways in the modern world.

JANET SAVED MANY YEARS to buy her own lovely sailboat, a 22 Square Meter, designed some eighty years ago by a Swede. It is long, low and powerful, and as a sailor might say, "easily driven." Some boats take time to find their groove. This one sets into it naturally, like a train on tracks. Janet gently grasps a long ash tiller connected to a small rudder at the trailing edge of a deep long keel.

The 22 Square Meter boats are strong enough for the big waves and big winds of the Baltic Sea, and at the same time have the horsepower to handle the fluky light air around the Swedish Archipelago. These design features and sailing performance combine to give Janet the sensation of ultimate precision and infinite flexibility, and a bit of Scandinavian history, when she drives.

She nudges the helm and the boat goes elsewhere. The tiniest course adjustments reveal subtle new speeds. Driving with a full suit of sails for any amount of time challenges her intellectual stamina, and when there are any waves to contend with, her athletic skill and physical strength as well. Janet likens it to flying a stunt plane, driving an Italian race car or making music on a handmade Martin guitar.

When her crew-mates raise the sails for the first time and she pushes the bow down to catch the wind, Janet never misses the rush of wonder that such a thing can happen at all.

Once in the groove, Janet stays by playing silent mind games. She times her breathing with the rhythm of the oncoming waves. The expansion of her shoulders and chest provide the background motive force for the slight tiller movements that she makes. She concentrates on feeling weather helm[22], as if measuring the pulse of the boat. In many conditions the boat can be sculled, weaving a long "S" curve on which Janet slightly turns away from the wind to reveal extended periods of subtle acceleration, and then

---

22 Weather helm is a light resistance, felt when holding a tiller of a sailboat in motion. Too much is slow, too little is uninformative.

turning back toward the wind gradually bleeds off the captured speed.

As a whole, the "S" shape she is steering is faster than an "I" shape would be. Sometimes the "S" can be a couple miles long and last for 20 or 30 minutes, so the turns are imperceptible to anyone but Janet. After an hour of driving, she's mentally exhausted, but completely aware that she has just been granted another hour of fullest living.

It takes two others to make Janet's privilege a reality. The boat is too powerful to sail alone. There are too many jobs to do, too far away from one another. Someone else muscles the big sails up and down. Someone else muscles them back and forth across the boat from tack to tack or jibe to jibe. Someone else muscles the long spinnaker pole and all the wind contained in the spinnaker around the front of the boat when they sail downwind. Someone else manages all the lines and loads that hold up the sails and the mast.

When this work isn't demanding their time, the crew must push and squish their bodies toward the outer edges of the boat, into undignified and damp places to keep the boat upright and fast. These are not design flaws. It was the designer's intent to create a platform on which a cohesive and cooperative team of people would work together.

When Janet drives, she often remarks aloud that she is the most privileged soul on earth at that moment. And she is serious. The team that affords her such a privilege, she suspects, understands her to be authentically grateful. She still worries that they may not be awash in the same sense of wonder that she feels when she drives.

So she takes deliberate steps to share the Grand Benefits by sharing the helm. Her intuition is that friendship comes from generosity, experience comes from doing and freedom comes from a combination of power and personal responsibility. To make sure, everyone on Janet's boat drives. But it's more than just steering.

When Janet nudges Anne, it is with the confidence rooted in a vast library of memories that stretch back at least to Ernie's outrigger canoe and probably earlier. In the present, Anne is not learning only by listening to Janet's stories. She is also having her own experiences — descended in a direct line from the Warszawaz Sailing Club's early explorations — but improved, colored and refined by the company around her and by modernity.

But Janet is rare. Most sailors don't embrace mentoring like she has, but instead rely on old business or military management models to crew and direct their boats.

Yacht-club bar talk claims that the best-run sailboats are those with a detail-obsessed benevolent dictator in charge, caring for the illiterate slog with extra rations of grog when earned, and bellowing, "Give me the helm, I'll find wind!"

after an hour in the doldrums, to the toothless crew's reverential applause. This happens in the movies, and signals, of course, that the crew's experiences need not be as rich.

Movie screens and sailors who are also active in business often try to apply business lessons to the lessons of sailing, and vice versa. Sometimes the metaphor works, sometimes it is a long stretch. It can even be badly flawed and self-destructive. Movie-think is usually shallow-think. Business-think is often charter-think. Neither works well when building a strong family.

If you have attended a workshop about leadership or business management or about sailboat racing, you might be familiar with the multi-layered pyramid that represents management and communication in groups. It shows strategy and the decision-maker at the top, tactics in the middle and timing and execution (the crew) at the bottom.

Using this shrink-wrapped management consultant framework, sailing schools often teach that success can only be achieved if a team first masters maneuvers, then boat speed, and then tactical decision-making. The message is that winning requires mastery of all three disciplines, but that they flow from the top down. In the end, many sailors have embraced what is essentially a hierarchical, closed organizational style.

Imposing a traditional hierarchy is as sinister to sailing as charter thinking, because it raises a large barrier to shared Grand Benefits.

In the hierarchy, the sailing skipper starts with and retains the right to evaluate and make every choice. Before skippers can do as much choosing as they would like, they must delegate the work of boat management to others who will think less and get to the job with some degree of coordination.

Unilateralism always weakens groups. Messages that cascade through layers are usually unclear or late arriving. When the flow of information slows on a racing sailboat, the result is usually a loss. Moreover, it is always a crummy time for the participants.

Imagine for a moment, a musical protégé held to the literal replay of a piece of music. She'd sooner quit than be chained to it. Now, imagine sailing spouses and their three teen daughters working together in a confined space; wet, cold and under pressure. Dad first patronizes with, "Let me help you, dear." Then, when frustrated, he barks expletive-laced commands in his best pirate voice. The sailing experience fails before launch.

I see the caricature of an old-school music teacher and a similar method: Start with technique (where to place your fingers). Move to repetition and speed (do your scales, do your scales, do your scales). And, finally, add some color through dynamics. Real thinking comes only at the end, and then, it is centered only at the top of the relationship hierarchy.

Finally, imagine a bright, motivated student like Danny, who has invested years in sailing lessons and competes at the collegiate level, invited to join a crew of a boat run by an old man who wants to be wise, but does not have the experience or reflexes to find the groove and shouts directives from behind the wheel, missing everything that Danny sees but is not authorized to announce. When there is not a commitment to collective fun, there can't be the dynamics that cement the long relationships, the personal satisfaction and joy that together become the Grand Benefits.

So we are left with kids who learn how to finger a piano but not to play it, and with shrinking fleets of floating kidless monarchies plying our bays.

As a footnote, recent research suggests that collective fun is far more important to competitiveness in sport than any other factor, including repetitive rehearsals. Collective fun easily translates to teamwork.

Sailors on sailboats where information flows openly, where the lessons of speed, maneuvers, navigation and tactics are always in view and are used as a basis for improvement, are far more likely to be enriched by the experience than sailors who have a job and a spot and are not part of the discussion.

Groups of people, including families, that interchangeably split and share roles and thinking will always benefit from a unifying group commitment to the process of finding new information and experiences. Then they collaborate to construct something bigger with it.

Group effort is not to be confused with group-think. It is not that they waste time seeking consensus every time, although sometimes they might find it.

Instead, everyone is part of both the planning and the post-op evaluation, so that the team understands the consequences of the team's decisions and their own contributions. Over time, the team accumulates a body of knowledge that is far greater than any one "decider" might be able to retain and process. For a teenager, these open discussions and visible, real consequences can only instill self-confidence, skill, pride and context.

Since information flows freely, everyone is more informed and more involved, willing to take a risk, more interested, and more emotionally connected. Most importantly, when a team of people works in concert, the fun flows seamlessly through it, and riding on top of the fun is the Grand Benefit. And finally, we get devotion.

Such simple interpersonal transactions might seem obvious, but they are not. The charter teaches us to expect entertainment, not to expect a deep experience, and so we don't often expect to *do,* but only to *receive.* Moreover, we almost never expect to do things in concert with others. This is why a boat ride, either in the form of basic training or a charter, doesn't make a sailor.

Sailors are made when other sailors offer ideas, debate issues and when they collaborate to get work done and to solve problems. Sailors are made when other sailors share nuanced experiences and bits of history to put the effort into perspective, like the glory of sculling a 22 Square Meter along a three-mile long "S."

CHAPTER 23

Modern Sailing

New world, new ways. How and why sailing will matter again.

FIRST BECAME AWARE OF a decline in sailing participation starting in the late 1980s. I began informal study of the issue in the late 1990s, and then, starting roughly in 2003, engaged in formal research to understand what was causing it.

I collected data and interviewed sailors and sailor wannabes and looked for the obvious. I asked sailors questions like "What prevents you from sailing?" . . . "How often do you sail?" . . . "What do you get from sailing?" . . . and "Would you do more sailing if . . . ?"

Especially among those who were non-sailors, I expected

to find perceptions of high costs, elements of elitism, and a fear of the unknown. I found little of any of that.

Instead, I mostly found people who said they wanted to sail but couldn't because they felt that they lacked the time. I would hear things like, "It's too big a commitment," and "I can't be gone from my family so long."

What the research has confirmed is a shift in time use and family dynamics over about thirty years that, for many, feels a bit like quicksand. The more they struggle in it, the more trapped they are. Sailing, it appears, falls prey to a larger, more daunting issue.

For a time I relented, thinking facts to be facts, and concluding that there just is not enough time for sailing and so it must go the way of a fad. I didn't see many solutions to the time-trap. Still, hoping that this would not be the end of the story, I looked for a hole in my research.

It was right in front of me.

I am as busy as ever. I work long hours. I travel for business. I have kids with homework and hobbies. Yet I almost never have difficulty finding the time for sailing, because — epiphany! — I am not leaving my family on shore. Both of my daughters sailed weeks after birth. For almost a decade, my wife and I strapped a child's car-seat and a sunbrella on the stern rail every summer weekend. We took infants and toddlers on overnight passages. We reconfigured a berth into a safe and soft playpen. We sailed on vacations and holidays. We sailed on weekends and weeknights. When out-of-town friends and family visited, we sailed. We sailed. We still sail.

I didn't have a problem with time because we sailed together. If we include our kids and spouses in our dreams, then our kids and spouses share our dreams. Time becomes the family's advantage, the fundamental ingredient in the life we share. The family becomes a memory machine.

Today, my wife and I have the rare privilege among parent peers of spending nearly every summer weekend and many summer evenings with our teenage daughters. We have common sailing friends of all ages, genders and backgrounds. We share common goals. We confront common challenges. And in the winter, when the boat is on blocks, we talk about how lucky we all are.

To be frank, serendipity granted us four other built-in advantages:

1. We live near the water.

2. Both my wife and I had long before deliberately unsubscribed from the charter and subscribed instead to shared time.

3. Early in our relationship, we were lucky to have friends that sailed to help both of us learn and who exposed us to the idea of family sailing, and so . . .

4. We were ready to involve our kids right away.

So we are left with the last few parts of the problem to consider. What is the ultimate make-up of the group that will sail? Can sailing begin with real novices, or does it require a lineage of experience? If it starts with the family, will it ever reach more than blood relatives? How far will it reach? Certainly, once the group forms, it will share powerful, intimate feelings. How might newcomers agree to do such a thing in the first place? Will they? Can anyone be excluded from it?

This book suggests that culture is created and transferred generationally through a continuum of mentoring that thrives only when people choose to spend meaningful and productive time with each other. We build the case that this continuum is currently broken and that it should be repaired to restore richness to our cultural and social identity. It identifies the family as a logical and powerful point of ignition.

What it has not said, at least not overtly until now, is that sailing isn't gender-neutral or age-neutral yet. But the society in which some young sailors like Anne and Sammy and Abigail are coming of age is far more open, diverse, longer-reaching and inclusive than any in human history. This is due in part to the daring and resolve of people like Ernie, Vince, Janet, Karl and Miss Morgan, who all stretched and bypassed false gender, age, ethnic and creative limits. They show us that a real Lifeline is not exclusive to fathers and sons. It can and must be as strong between fathers and daughters, mothers and sons, grandmothers and teenagers, blue collar and white collar, educated and not. Culture can't be age, race, bloodline or gender exclusive, and neither can sailing.

Let's face it. The vast majority of today's American sailors are white men, aged 45 to 65 years old, like me. As much as I would like to call us in this category culturally enlightened, I am afraid that we middle-aged male sailors of mostly Western European descent will not recreate the Lifeline on our own. But we can play an important role if we choose it.

Recall Larry and his boats and his distant non-sailing family. Larry is not antisocial, a racist, a sexist nor an isolationist. He has just checked out. He's in that stage in life. He thinks his best chance to help to create a Lifeline is behind him, and he has acknowledged as much with his choices. His kids are gone and he has decided, right or wrong, that he does not play a role in such things anymore. By choosing to reminisce on the water instead of mentoring, he is *also choosing to let the time pass.*

If he or others like him read this, I hope he will see that it need not be so. Cultural enlightenment includes knowing that one can play a part in our culture at any time in one's life, and with anyone in our social network. The active role is available. What he needs to do is choose it.

Larry can become a mentor-parent even now. As long as he is still here, he can reach out to his kids and theirs to teach them what he knows about sailing, and through it, what he knows about the world. If that isn't realistic due to timing or distance, he has ample supply of neighbors and friends with kids and grandkids.

If Larry sails with someone younger, it will be because he has bravely faced and is determined to cross a wide generational gap. He might find that he doesn't understand as much about sailing or about kids as he would like, or that it is hard for him to relate to the modern interests of youth. While he has the tools that he needs to sail on his terms, he'll have to be open to the new ways that kids approach sailing and the exciting new tools that they prefer. For a time it might seem more frightening than learning to sail alone. In the same way and with a bit of time invested, he'll become more familiar and more confident. The fear will fade and be replaced with satisfaction as rich or richer than any nostalgia.

Beyond Larry and his peers, recall Jeanne and her mixed feelings as her husband went on a sailboat buying-bender without her. She must have felt unfamiliar, anxious, stressed, fearful, inadequate and even sad all at once. Today she certainly views the ordeal as a costly mistake. Also recall Danny's mom, who had the job of delivering Danny to lessons and races, but never got much out of it herself and missed out on some important parenting years. Counter these experiences with those of Calayag, sailing while raising young T.J.

We can't dance around the role of women and specifically of mothers and the task of mothering in the mentor-parent discussion. In fact, we should address it head on.

To do that, let's plot social value delivered from sailing, using a range of common and not-so-common sailing situations that have developed over time. Here we can see why sailing has been mostly about men and boys in the past (and can see our way to modernizing sailing by integrating it with parenting, regardless of gender).

1. *A father and son sail together.* Of course, this is the way it was done most often at sailing's peak of popularity in the late 1970s. It not only multiplied the number of sailors for a time, it instilled the devotion that still exists today among aging male boomers. But for the most part, women and girls stayed onshore.

2. *A boat sailed by one.* This happens because others haven't agreed or haven't been asked. It is what Larry does. We're left to think that a time-choice opportunity has been lost for a bunch of people. And here, too, for the most part, Larry's peers are men.

3. *One kid in a sailboat, sailing against other kids, each in their own boat.* In pure competition we value this structure for the levelness of the playing field. But organized sports, including sailing, traditionally tend to separate kids along gender lines due to physical differences. In this structure, social value comes mostly in the preparation period when a mentor-parent (or a good coach) is the sparring partner or the guide. And when the coaches are men, they tend to spar with other men.

4. *A crewed sailboat on which friends sail together.*
Here, sailing might mix competition or adventure with a social event like a party or a picnic, and gender lines blur for a time. But if crewmates leave their respective families onshore too long, something will eventually have to give. Today, for every seven sailors on a boat, only one is a woman and almost none of these are active mothers. When people mature, pair-up and start having kids, sailing can't remain a priority. Unless . . .

5. *A family — a parent or parents, with daughters, sons, and the family's friends — sail together.*

It is in this last situation that we can see the Life Pastime in all its glory: Grand Benefits in full bloom. Shared experiences spark memories in all directions. It is the formula that provides relief to the parent who has been left out, whose role was taxi-driver and cheerleader. It is the environment that provides substance beyond entertainment to every participant. It is the setting that reflects, emphasizes and taps the modern roles of women and men, wives and husbands, young and old.

It is also the way that single parents, all too common these days, can step onto the mentoring continuum — what we've called the Lifeline — and manage more than just the day-to-day holding together of a household. In fact, sailing together (or singing, or fishing or sewing) may be an excellent way to hold the family together.

Not a subscription to some program. Not a matter exclusive to anyone, but instead, an array of overlapping social commitments: individuals offering to reach inward and discover and share authentic, contagious enthusiasm, along with a group-wide covenant to use all the strength in all the relationships to reach out into the world. When sailing finally includes whole families and their networks, then sailing will gain in popularity again because it will matter again.

Think about Anne, mother of two, third in a line of gender-blind mentors, setting an example for the next in line. We have seen that Anne is not just up to it, she is engaged in it, motivated by it, and living because of it.

I heard one mentor-parent sailing mother say, "We want to teach these kids that they can do anything in their lives. What example does it set for them if I drive away? Yeah, it's cold and wet and on some days, I'd rather be somewhere else. But I'm not, and they see it."

And she paused and thought for a minute, and added,

"And on those rare days when it all comes together — warm, sunny, breezy, teamwork — well, then we all get a big bonus, don't we?"

Like Larry's challenge to step over a wide generational chasm, Anne's choice to sail is equally bold. She does things not long ago thought to be reserved for men, and she doesn't do the things thought to be required of women today.

It is in the end a question of leadership, with mentors like Anne choosing to lead by teaching and apprentices like Anne's children aspiring to lead when their time comes. Or potential mentors like Larry seeing beyond tired, old gender and age gaps, to find new apprentices that deserve his time for reasons bigger than him. Leadership isn't something we can make; it is a self-fulfilling state of being, a time when we are aware of both today's reality and tomorrow's potential.

To balance the now with the next, leaders see change as constant and inevitable, and progress as its product.

Good leaders, of course, are honest leaders. They know that if sailing is to be popular, they must not promise that it is simple when it obviously isn't. If something is perceived to be hard, and it is indeed hard, then leaders tell the truth: It is hard, and *that's what makes it good.*

Anne has learned, as a musician, teacher, mother, mentor-parent and sailor, that *hard things matter* and that *hard things done in groups matter most.* So she confronts the challenge, and challenges others to confront it too.

And she knows why: It's not all about her. It's about her family, and the decisions that she makes, and that they make together, that affect them all. From the vantage point of her own choices, she can see that it is also about other people's families, both in the present, the past and especially in the future. Anne knows that she's part of the continuum. *So Anne matters.*

Cultural enlightenment, arguably the deepest insight of a leader, is the sense that one's role in culture is larger than one's life or longer than one's lifetime. It is the ability to recognize an earthly time horizon that is far beyond one's own.

Grand Benefits return on a generational scale. They influence and cross over all the present barriers we have witnessed here. Often they are so Grand, that we can't grasp them fully but can only sense that they are there, like butterflies landing on a twig of a massive oak tree, or like crewmates on a tiny sailing boat miles from shore.

In order for sailing to matter we must shift our perspective about its role in culture. Larry has always seen sailing as a way of looking backward. Anne sees it as a way of honoring the past, but looking forward. The other mentors in our stories do too.

For this, we return to a cold, rainy Sunday morning about fifty years ago. Janet, her best high-school girlfriend Calayag and Janet's dad Ernie treaded water, gasping and hollering as big green waves broke over and around them and pieces of yellow Thistle floated by. They had gone left and were too close to Turtle Island when the boat came off a wave and dropped onto a rock, blowing apart around them.

For the first few seconds, it seemed as if rescue would be impossible. The sea-state was treacherous and the water was cold enough to induce hypothermia, if they could stay on the surface. Janet was shaken but confident. She and Ernie had practiced this over and over. She inhaled between waves, exhaled into the knotted sleeves of her foulies, kicked off her boots and forced herself to relax into the tiny bit of buoyancy that she had made for herself.

Calayag, on the other hand, was panicked and was catching big mouthfuls of water. Ernie made a choice. He visually checked on Janet, then grabbed the oilskin lunch-sack as it floated by and swam behind Calayag. He wrapped his strong arm around her chest and shoulders and firmly pulled her onto his hip to lever her head higher out of the water with a side stroke. He pressed the lunch-sack into Calayag's hands and told her to squeeze it to her stomach. It was zippered tight and held a bit of air.

Between waves he signaled Janet to keep waving to the rest of the fleet but to stay near. Then he began to quietly talk about whether lunch would be dry or soggy and the ride home and what time the race would start next week. Calayag's panic subsided. After what seemed like hours but was only minutes, Ernie and Janet teamed to help Calayag over the transom and into Walter's bucking Thistle and then, together, they climbed aboard opposite sides of Francis' boat.

In bed that night Ernie broke into a cold sweat, thinking about the horrible things that might have happened. He felt terrible. He had known the shoal was dangerous. He had known the weather was awful. Worst of all, he had left his daughter to fend on her own. Maybe he was risking too much with these kids. He got up for some warm milk and an aspirin. Janet met him at the refrigerator and gave him a reassuring hug.

In the morning before school and work, Calayag brought Ernie a thermos of hot cocoa with a big red bow and a thank-you card from her mom, written in the Filipino alphabet and illegible to Ernie. At Walter's insistence, they sailed again the next week in Walter's boat, while Walter and crew took over as race committee.

On a glistening sunny Sunday, Janet, Calayag and Ernie put on new lifejackets, port-tacked the Thistle fleet and came in second last, but couldn't stop talking about what it was like swimming and fearing in cold, gray Lake Erie. Janet admitted that she was more afraid than she had let on. Calayag teared up a couple of times thinking about Ernie's calm bravery. Ernie tried hard to make sense of the contrast: terror last week, euphoria this.

Ernie offered the helm to Calayag halfway through the race. As they rounded the Toledo Harbor Light on the last leg, golden sun beaming, silver water glistening and rainbow-colored spinnaker drawing, Calayag proclaimed, "This is *the finest place on earth!* Why would anyone choose to be anywhere else today?"

And then she added, "Thanks, Mr. Lipinski, for sharing it with me."

At that moment, Ernie resolved that in the end, he would be buried at sea at the Toledo Harbor Light, just rightly deemed the finest place on earth by a neighborhood kid with a funny accent. In the now, he would never choose to let the time pass. Instead, he would face down the risks and do and share the things that matter.

Today Anne's two children are connected to Calayag only by the wakes of their small sailboats crossing fifty years apart. They'll never know her, where she came from or that she called it first. Still, young Abigail and Sammy sense something Grand when they reach out their toes to try to touch the finest place on earth. Anne watches and smiles and then gets ready to tail the jib on the next tack for her friend and mentor Janet.

Memories made.

CHAPTER 24

Conclusion: Action Plan

Yes we can and should save sailing and the other things that matter — things like childhood, the family, long friendships, rich experiences and real freedom — by choosing to use our time wisely.

"So what do we do now, Nick?" asked my sailing friend and draft-edition editor, Tim Kent. "I agree with what you're saying, but how can we make improvements?"

I replied, "Tim, I did not write this to promote sailing. My conclusion is that you can't make time choices for people. They have to make their own choices."

Tim was unrelenting. "Yes, but we have almost two million sailors, another million that want to be, and three hundred sailing clubs that all want to share what they know is so great about sailing. How can we help them to play a role in building a better society?"

I thought for a minute.

"All right," I said, "let's write a simple action plan for anyone who wants to use it. Heck, if a folk musician wants to use it to start to build a folk music legacy, all he or she needs to do is replace some words."

Tim agreed.

So here I close with some specific ideas on how to rescue the Life Pastime. First, some things that any person can do, starting with a few basic ideas:

Mentor someone!

- Never let the time pass. Instead, use it to qualify as a mentor. Master something, and then . . .

- Share it. Use whatever it is to help the next generation of apprentices become mentors themselves. And watch it take on a larger meaning for everyone involved.

- Start now.

NICHOLAS D. HAYES

There are things that any family can do, beginning with a commitment to recover wasted time by making some smarter time choices. Bold steps may be required:

- Live where and in a way that the family isn't separated most of the time.

- Build schedules that value and create overlapping free time, and find something to do together during it. Perhaps sailing.

- Form or join a club with people who share a common interest instead of subscribing to cable television.

- Never confuse team sports with teamwork. One is fun. The other is family fun.

- Never confuse peak performance with growth and learning. One matters for a few years, the other matters for a lifetime.

ᐁ

Organizations and associations have a role:

1. Define "family friendly" not as something sanitized or segregated, but as a thing purposely built for active family use. Clubs, boats, classes and curriculum should be gender and age neutral. Schedules must accommodate the realities of family life and the cooperation of groups.

2. Instead of creating programs where kids are dropped off and picked up by parents, parent participation should be a prerogative. Youth sailing schools should be redesigned to actively enlist parents or guardian adults, as equal participants and eventually as mentors. Such a thing can start simply. For example, the Milwaukee Community Sailing Center has a new kids' class with a built-in parent day that will be expanded into a class for both parents and kids; it will eventually evolve into a families-only, family team sailing series.

3. Organizations like clubs and schools should be designed to help mentors find apprentices and

vice versa — and to sequence risk and learning for everyone, across age groups and skill levels, without getting in the way of fun.

4. Clubs should float fleets of shared boats, carefully manage time, and offer easy access to the water, but not much more. Community centers should float fleets of renewed boats for public lessons and use.

An action plan can't be a good tool without a list of things to avoid.

1. Don't focus on making entry easy; instead create open access and let the benefits pull those who choose to participate.

2. Don't encourage sailing, or for that matter any Life Pastime, to be a spectator sport. It's bad for sailing and for spectators.

3. Never outsource leadership. Leaders are a product of time invested and shared experiences. So

invest time and share experiences among leaders and potential leaders.

4. Don't think that schools or programs or clubs can do what parents and/or mentors should do. And don't assume parents or teachers can do something that they are untrained for or unfamiliar with. Parents, teachers (even teachers in sailing schools) and students are part of the same team, but have different roles.

5. Never separate families and friends.

6. Never limit access to the water or deny someone time on a sailboat.

List of Tables

About the Author

Nick Hayes has studied sailing, sailors and sailing clubs for years, interviewing more than 1,200 sailors worldwide since 2003 in preparation to write this book. He is a partner at the consulting firm FiveTwelve Group, where he helps businesses learn about markets, customers and value.

He lives in Shorewood, Wisconsin with his wife Angela and their two daughters, all decorated sailors. The Hayes family campaigns their B-32 sailboat *Syrena* out of the South Shore Yacht Club and sail together for fun as often as they can.

Nick currently serves on the Board of Directors of the Milwaukee Community Sailing Center, chairing its Program Committee and teaching courses in crew development and advanced sail-trim. He is also active on the Youth Sailing Committee of the South Shore Yacht Club, and spent four years as a director and was the Fleet Captain of the Milwaukee Yacht Club.